LIMINAL: Belief

A Collection of Stories

LIMINAL
Published by Stain'd INC
1172 York St. Denver, CO
80206

StaindMagazine.com

For permissions contact:
support@StaindMagazine.com

ISBN 978-1-948850-01-8

Cover by Hattie Rensberry

Systems of belief are inevitably built around narrative and story, which is to say that most things we feel connected to are. We crave to hear not just what is *known* but also, and maybe more significantly, what has *happened*. Even the most theoretical understandings must be confirmed by the story the speaker tells about the past—and the faith, hope, or belief they have for what will happen in the future—all bound up in the passage of time, in the existence of characters, and in the power of place.

As someone curious about language, it always interested me to see how many things narrative finds its way in to, and yet so little attention is given to the crafting or receiving of a good story. But spend a moment sitting in a crowded dining hall, in a classroom of any kind, a café or bar, around a kitchen table, a bed shared between lovers and you will hear stories. Every place—a setting, every person—a character. Sit in your living room alone on a Friday night, uncertain where you belong, and there too you have a story, filled with all the potential as any other.

Politicians practiced in new and tired tales of heroism and villainy; actors in our halls of justice trained in its art—even scientists can't help when connecting with people to fall into the grand dramas of rock and water, particles personified in their dance with one another.

Story helps us make connections. It is to know how elements interact, how environment shapes those elements, and how those elements shape their environment. It is to know how it was for them, to be allowed to live in some small way that which the story teller has lived—that which they have understood, to know it ourselves. To allow those mirror neurons a full heartmind fire. To be made bigger by the sum of our experiences.

Liminal: A Storytelling Event took place on a Saturday night in March at the Mercury Café draped in its rainbow curtains to a sitting and standing room. Eight storytellers were asked to explore what came to mind when given the word: Belief.

If you try and think of what comes to mind as one is likely to do, you might feel it challenging. The mind struggles to find its symbols. What, if I had to say it, if I were to show it, is it that I believe?

Profoundly personal and political, belief plays an elusive but supremely influential role in shaping our lives—the fragmented, shared make-believe that the modern man and woman must participate in, in order to join together. It is something we aren't even always conscious of—belief almost, oftentimes, transcends thought. It buries itself somewhere in our bones.

These storytellers were tasked with sharing something that informed this idea. To explore what drives us. You will find here the text of those stories.

We gathered there, as we do here, to celebrate the art of the story, the drama and comedy of the people's moment, to peek behind the curtain, to take stock of what has happened and to see what can be found in it. What words, of all those words, might tell me what I believe, which ones and in what order might tell the world?

Noah Kaplan,
Artistic Director
Stain'd Arts

Liminal (lim-i-nal):
occupying a position at, or on both sides of, a boundary or threshold.

The LIMINAL series is an experiment in pushing audiences to the edge of their comfort zones through the art of storytelling. Within this book are true stories told live at our inaugural event. Stories about belief in the self, belief in a higher power, and belief in the unknown. Storytellers talked about the barriers that we face to fully step into our beliefs, they talked about what it takes to leave behind toxic beliefs that may have surrounded us in our youth. We hope throughout this book you contemplate the question, "what do you believe in?" LIMINAL strives to celebrate difference and push ourselves to challenge our own assumptions. Enjoy these stories, the art, and the community voices held within this book.

Included within this book are illustrations sketched live during each of the ten minute stories, from artist Alex Baldoz.

The LIMINAL series is part of an ongoing collaboration with Soul Stories, a story-based organization that hosts events, workshops and spaces to promote healing, empowerment, and social connectedness through a community-building framework that addresses challenging topics impacting local communities. Soul Stories believes that a common thread between all humans can be established by facilitating communication and the disclosure of our human experience. By facilitating understanding, connection and respect within the context of our differences, we have the potential to build communities that support the acceptance of everyone across racial, gender, sexual identity, and other differences.

Stain'd is a non-profit which creates platforms for an intersectional community of artists to explore subversive topics and present provocative work based on the philosophy that art which challenges held beliefs is art doing its best service in society. Stain'd seeks to offer the world unfamiliar representations of beauty. Through the use of community events, publishing, and workshops all focused around the arts we support the growth of a radically compassionate space to share what might otherwise be kept secret; build connection; explore difficult, nuanced topics without fear; and show the common concept made new.

The Ghosts I Live With

Written By: Rachel Trignano

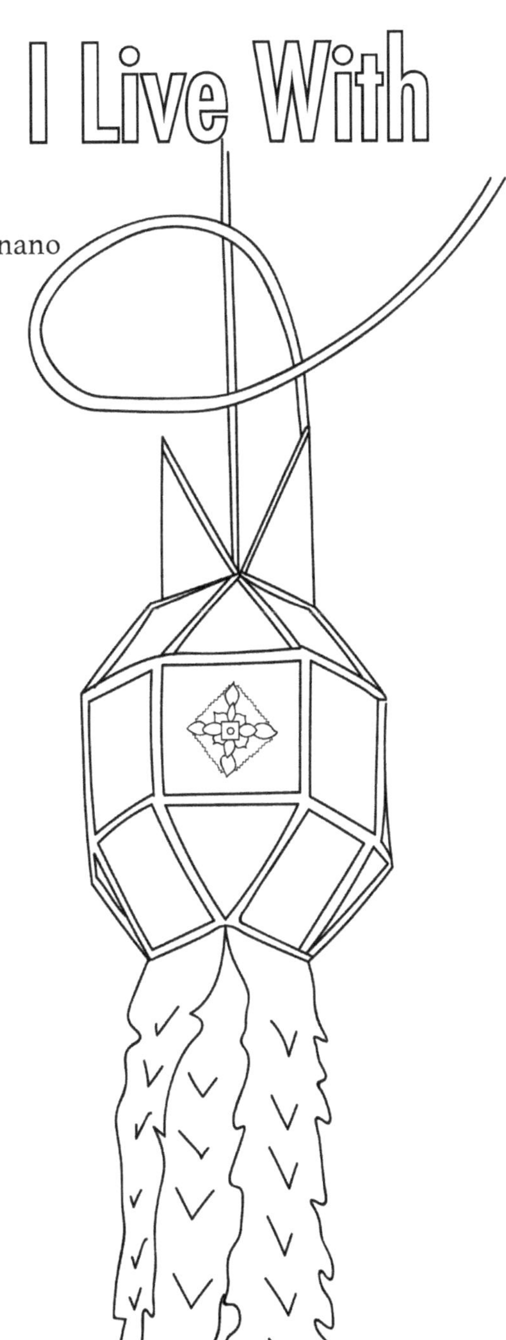

W hen we are children, ghost stories are as tantalizing as they are terrifying because there is a threat of legitimacy. We turn them from tall tales into replicable premonitions, and, paradoxically, want them to be both.

People ask me if I believe in ghosts, and, of course, I do: I grew up in a very small, very haunted house back east. Haunted by whose ghosts, I don't know. I knew they weren't mine, which is to say: I didn't want them. To be fair, I don't think they wanted me, either.

There was always the fear of when the next one would appear — when their watchfulness would press into the nape of my neck or I'd hear them murmuring downstairs long after the TV sets had cooled and I could hear my stepfather snoring. The ghosts were with me while I played with my dolls, or as I walked up the stairs to my room. It wasn't until high school that I stopped taking our stairs sideways with my back to the wall, an a-scared Fred Astaire sliding my shoulder blades against the wallpaper as one foot over the other sunk into the carpet.

As someone who often saw, heard, or felt the dead and their variants, I was a very poor sleeper. Yet the one ghost that brought me the most unrest was my father's — not because I could see it, but because I couldn't.

My father was a young man when he died, just a few weeks shy of his 29th birthday. I wasn't given the details of how it happened until I was old enough to hear them, but I don't think there is such an age. His death was sudden and gruesome and, I've decided in more recent years, offensively undignified. To his wife and parents, it was a horrific tragedy. To me, a young child, it was as true as any other ghost story, which is to say: very possibly so.

I was only a year and a half old when my father died, my sister just two years older. He wasn't much in my memory, and my life carried on without commotion after he was gone. At that age, death is an impermanent inconvenience. You are told someone is not coming back, but that's presumably of the dead's own volition. With this thinking, death is, at its worst, a selfish failing to be available to the living.

Despite the many ghosts I reluctantly roomed with, my fa-

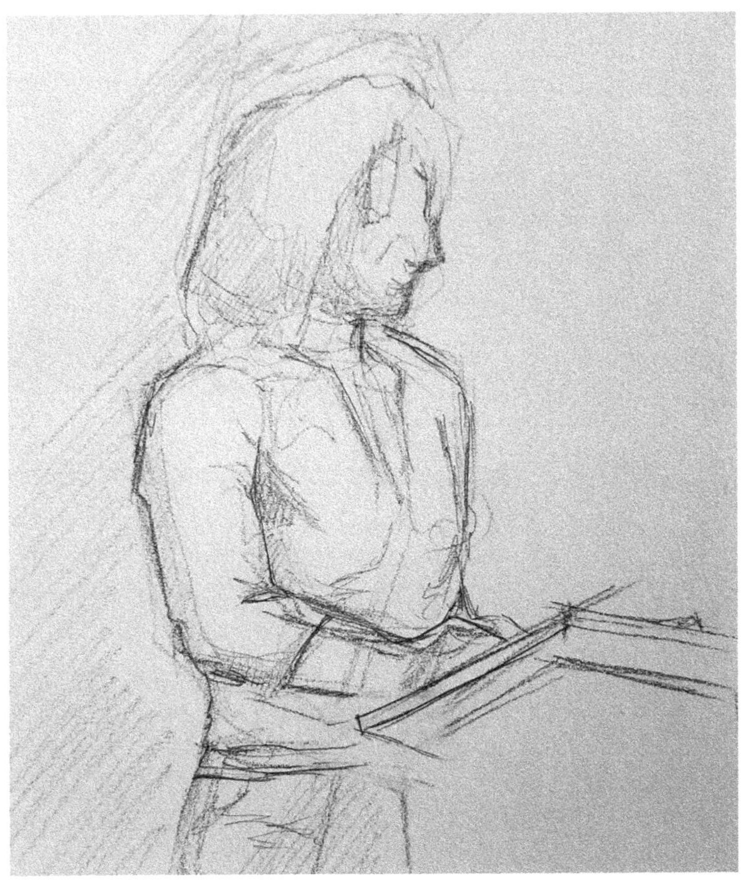

ther's never appeared. He always seemed near, as if he was on the other side of a wall, waiting with waning patience for me to find him. I would wait for him to appear — will him to appear — but years went by and he remained an absent apparition. That would become his greatest failing in my eyes: not that he had left us, but that he stubbornly would not return.

As words came to me, so did questions. "Where is he?" and "When is he coming back?" achieved the same answers, which were too frustrating and then, later, too sad to be asked again. My questions became more thoughtful over time as I removed myself as the lens through which I needed to observe him. "What was he like?" "What did he eat?" "What did he watch on TV?"

There is perhaps no hungrier audience than that of a ghost story: every revelation is a disappointment, and every disappoint-

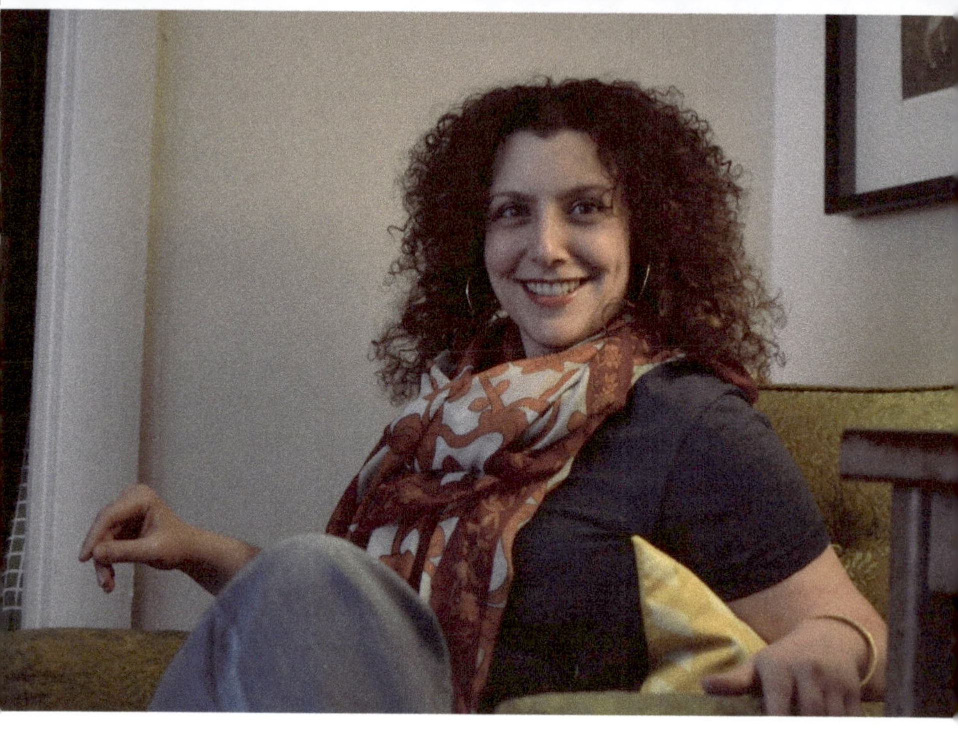

ment breeds a need for a greater revelation. As I tried to piece togeth-er my father's existence, my two most prolific, if not reliable, resources were my mother (wife and widow) and his father (creator and, in some ways, destroyer). My grandmother's memories of him, like the rest of her memories, were blurred through the bottoms of monogrammed barware. I left them to their watery graves.

My grandfather's mind, on the other hand, was talon-sharp — but his ego gave him a weakness for well-turned lies: Truth was always a blemish to be concealed and corrected. By his recount, there was no one more handsome, intelligent, or forthright than my father — my father, the junior college dropout with a city job who spent more time unaccounted for than my mother liked in the months be-fore his death. My mother was worlds more honest than my grandfa-ther, but the fairness of her recollections were either warped by nos-talgia or hobbled by grief and resentment.

As time passed, their accounts of my father grew wildly more divergent from one another's. When I turned away from the blinding burnish of my grandfather's pretension, I was slapped with the pain of a woman who was as abandoned and bereft as I was. I started look-ing for my father on my own in the assorted ephemera that, like myself, had outlived him and been relocated into a cramped, cluttered home he would never visit.

As a young teenager, my mother gave me his record albums, which I still have and still play. Later on, I would acquire his yearbook. I would stare at the photo, his quixotic quote in a fussy, italicized serif under his colorless image: "It is good only if it is wild and free; but most of all, enjoy."

Other pictures of my father were rare and unedifying. In the hundreds of photographs my mother took, he appears sporadically, standing on a beach or napping in a rowboat — and, on one occasion, laughing. In most of his photos he allows an oblique half-smirk, the mask of a masculine inscrutability only a camera can provoke. Despite his being an apt marksman with a rifle, he was clearly not a fan of the household point-and-shoot. A chance photo he himself once took of his pocket watch near a note he wrote tells me I have a fairly frenetic version of his penmanship: capitalized, upright, sometimes dashed and disjointed. I think, in a way, I'm the fairly frenetic version of him. I wash his face and wave his hands. Smile with his dimples. Get my comb caught in his curly hair.

As I got older, family members were bewildered by how much I resembled him, and I started to learn more illuminating and uncanny similarities between us. We're both unflinchingly direct. We love Jimi Hendrix and motorcycles and candy bars, and our mouths crimp the same way when we drink a bottle of beer. We're brash and foolishly rebellious. Selfish and self-indulgent. Directionless. Adrift. As my identity solidified, so did his. It wasn't until I weathered enough of my own failings that I could accept his, and understand the difference between fucking up and being a fuck up. He hadn't failed us. He had just stopped being alive.

When I want to see his ghost now, I look in the mirror. His face is getting wrinkles. He's finding more grey hairs. Now that I'm seven years his senior, I've seen what 84 more months, 364 more weeks, 2,555 more days look like after you've gone: They look the same, the world moves on.

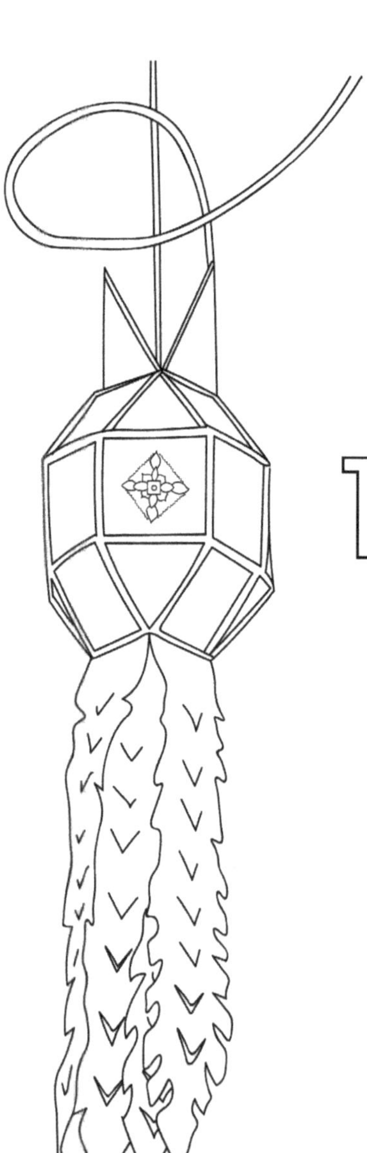

Shoulder To Shoulder

Written By: Jonathan Stalls

Our arms are swinging and the landscape is slowly moving alongside of us. The fresh Colorado air wraps itself around our cheeks, our breath, and our bodies. The sky is big and the air is dry and warm. It feels good to be outside, away from the walls. Our walking group finds itself every Thursday morning tucked in the concretecovered corners of Southeast Denver. For those that might be unfamiliar, Denver's large metropolitan area sits in what's called Colorado's Front Range. It lies directly in the middle of the flat Eastern Plains and the high Rocky Mountains. Most of the region is a product of post World War II sprawling suburban development considering much of its infrastructure boomed in the 1950's and 1960's. International markets, cafes, and service centers sprinkle the busy arterial streets surrounding the daycare center.

The women on this weekly walk are from Iraq. They are refugees and they came to the U.S. just after the U.S./Iraq war and are roughly all over the age of 60. It all started when I humbly entered the daycare center for the first time as the only English as a first language person in the room. I was invited to ask the women, supported by Arabic interpretation, if they would enjoy a weekly community walk to the nearby creek and perhaps other parks and trails. They said yes. So here we are. This is a partnership that's formed between our walking community, a local intercultural nonprofit, and an adult daycare center. We have a team of leaders who support the weekly walk and we also fundraise to help provide safe and comfortable walking shoes.

We aim to begin our walk in a sharing circle at the large tree just before our first busy road. We like to gather and share names, especially if there is someone new in the group. This walk is not open to the public as we are sensitive to the safety and comfort of the group. We do; however, invite people to join along on a one or two people at a time basis. It is so sad to me that we have to navigate and strongly consider segments of our culture where hijabs and refugees are not only unwelcome but considered a threat.

We're now walking, all nine of us, side by side. Some of us right next to each other, some holding hands, and others behind or in front. Humble glances and friendly smiles are exchanged. Most of the women carry previous conversations into a moving dialogue.

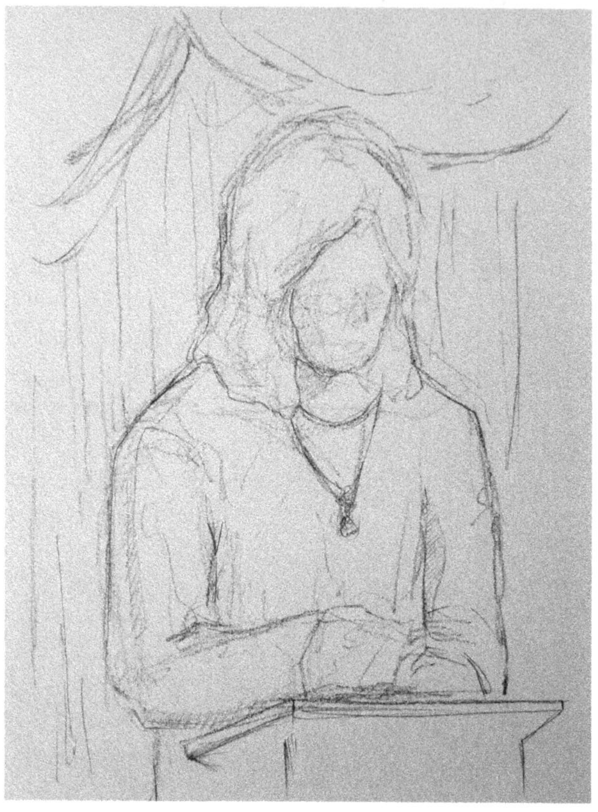

Some of the women hardly talk at all, if ever. We seem to subconsciously agree that there's enough in the outside world to keep our attention and our connection without words. We start our walks on a curvy highspeed road as the lack of sidewalks and blind spots give us no choice. I am on full alert for cars flying around the corner.

As I consider their physical safety from the speed of our roads, I also wonder how people behind their windshields or office windows process the sight of six or fifteen refugee women walking the streets together. We've made it so easy to stay isolated in our fixed thoughts and perspectives. Does a walk like this feed and fuel previous opinions and postures, or does a walk like this start to break them down? I am always hoping for spontaneous interactions between our beautiful walking group and the people who dart between their parked car and their destination.

That said, I also wonder if they were to strike up a conversation, would those who cross their path be open enough to listen, struggle with, and even hold what these amazing women might have to share?

Most of the women are Muslim and wear colorful or black hijabs. A few of them are Christians, many with strawberry blond colored hair. I try to always arrive early enough in time for breakfast. I'm blessed with whatever is available and it is such a joy to sit, with little words, and eat with this beautiful community. Arabic news stations come through the hanging televisions. The menu consists of long blocks of cheese, hardboiled eggs, fava beans, marinated cucumbers and tomatoes, yogurt, bagels and traditional Iraqi bread (or Khubz). One of my favorite things to witness is seeing the many different religious expressions sharing breakfast together at the same table. Their culture, their language, their foods and their traditions of home seem to bring them together beyond their different beliefs.

Most of these families fought on the side of the U.S. during the U.S. and Iraq war. Most of them have lost immediate loved ones in the war: sons, husbands, brothers, sisters and cousins... gone. Tears well up in their eyes, and in mine, every time it comes up on our walks. They are grateful to the U.S. for their role in the war; however, many of them miss the culture and roots of their homeland. They are angry and sad for the state of their home country and with gratitude, are doing whatever they can to make things work here in the U.S. I'll never forget two of the women coming up to me in early 2017 when our country had a ban on Iraqi refugees. They asked, "We are looking at places to go. We don't feel safe here in Colorado. We feel there are better states to live in. What do you think, Mr. Jonathon, would Oregon be better for us? Please tell us. We'll move. Do you know people in Oregon?" I had no answers for them. I was sad, angry, and humbled by the weight of their words. I so badly wished there were simply more people in our country living in relationship with these beautiful families to affirm that they are welcome here, right where they are.

We're still walking. Up and over broken sidewalks, ducking under pine trees and soaking in the warm rays of sun peering out through the surrounding office buildings. Without words we are still listening and connecting to one another. I can't speak Arabic and you can only say "How are you?", "What is new?" so many times the answer is met with a humble smile and a squint. We do however, connect around everything else. I pick up sticks, point out plants, encourage stretching motions, offer up dance shuffles, and more. We laugh and we move. Nature and one another's company feels good and it's always enough.

After having guided so many group walking experiences, I have utmost trust for what takes place when the body starts to move in this way. The fluids, the cells, and the neurons are given full permission to develop body rhythm, circulation, and coordination. With 26 bones, 33 articulations, 111 ligaments, and over 20 muscles in the feet alone this activity frees our most foundational elements to move and do what they were made to do[1].

I always show up with a wooden walking stick. The women always ask me why I have it. "You are young," they say. "Why do you have this? To protect us from the dogs?" they laugh and continue. They want to touch it and try it. They always find it to be an entertaining part of our journey together. In fact, as my hair grows past my shoulders I'm now getting welcomed as Thor and Jesus by the women and the men every time I walk into the daycare center. I feel blessed, in that strange way, to be a frequent target for a good late morning joke. The walks are helping us connect and build trust. It's subtle and playful. I find the freedom of this to be profound and I believe it has so much to do with the fact that we are, specifically, walking together. We're not inside of walls defaulting to our ability to keep a certain kind of conversation going. It's not as easy for us to stay huddled with our cliques around our usual tables. The outside world, our bodies and our movement, naturally allow for us to move in and out of conversation if desired.

The streets we walk are full of parking lots, wide roads, and tiny sidewalks that push us into traffic. It's no mystery why so many people give in to being sedentary and inside. Going at this alone or with one or two people can be a daunting task, especially as an older adult. We've done a sad and unfortunate job at pouring pavement over the softness of dirt, the glow of grasses, and the breath of trees.

We are all waiting and huddling at the fragile pedestrian island facing a big hightraffic intersection awaiting our great crossing to the Cherry Creek and all that grows and flourishes around it. The cars rush past us six lanes deep in all directions. It's plain frighten-

1 Rubinstein, Born to Walk, pg 15

ing when the fragile human frame is surrounded by masses of uneven concrete, highspeed automobiles eager to reach their destination, and traffic signals that offer only seconds to cross. I often see the women lock elbows and stand close together as one body. I am always overwhelmed with how sad it makes me feel that we've made our environments so hostile to moving this way.

We cross the street. I find myself breathing and reciting a quick blessing after we all make it safely. It's frightening, but the rewards are worth it. We continue walking up over a beautiful wooden bridge. The glow of the sun off the grasses is calming, no matter the season. Ducks and geese float along the approaching creek and the sound of the rushing water begins to compete with the noise of traffic.

We eventually make it to our bench near the rocks where the water rushes down into a small waterfall. The women know it and they have made it their own special destination to take a break. Some of the women, feeling energized, will go on a bit further and then turn back to take their break once the others catch up. On a warm, summer day we'll go all the way down to the water and allow the coolness of it to rush over our feet and hands. They love this and are always taking photos with one another to share with family and friends.

The first time I took the group, they were amazed. They had been going to the same adult daycare center for 8 years and they never knew this cozy and nurturing spot with running water was just a 15 minute walk away.

Life calls us to be in relationship to what is living around us. It calls us to mirror what is real and breathing between our own bodies and that of cottonwood trees, swimming muskrats, the faces and stories of those around us, and a mother and son walking by while holding hands. I believe life pleads for us to better ground our ideas of other and of creation based on more presence with and proximity to them. It seems we do so much harm when we base our ideas of other solely from our often narrow worldviews and adopted postures and positions.

From the touch of an ancient tree to the soft hand of an elder asking for help, life calls out to life. Are we unhurried enough to show up, to listen, and to be available to its call?

I'll never forget one of our first group walks all the way down to the water. We were relaxing and taking in the sun and sounds of nature. As we moved about, one of the women poured out her small paper cup of water and quietly tiptoed down the rocks to the cold creek. She held the cup with one hand and lifted her long skirt with the other. She kneeled and filled her small cup with the cold creek water. Having no care for her friend's dress and mall shoes, she came up from behind and began to pour water onto her head. The screams and the shock! Everyone's attention quickly focused on the woman who was now wet with creek water.

I was waiting for my first group fight or a good long laugh. She busted out laughing, thank everything. All the women roared and if it wasn't for some of her discomfort getting down the rocks, she would have surely returned the favor to her bold friend. We laughed the whole way back. The playfulness was magic.

Walking activity helps to bless, heal, and cleanse everything these women carry, physical and emotional. I see the transformation from start to finish every time. I'm hopeful that our walks remind them of their freedom and their connection to their body.

We made our way back to the daycare center. Many "thank yous" in English and in Arabic moved between us. The women would go right to the couches or the chairs to catch their breath and drink water. They were smiling and feeling energized. I've been told by the people in our partnership that this is one of the most valuable programs they have ever had.

Many of us lean into the idea that getting outside for some fresh air is a good thing. What I hope is considered when holding this story is the benefit and opportunity to take it a little further by adopting solo or group walking. This added layer of movement and connection can radically impact one's state of being. Whether family, friends, colleagues, or those we don't quite understand, this invitation to move together at an unhurried pace is ready to be used and held as a mechanism for how we go into deeper relationship with one another and the world around us.

Walks like these profoundly change me from the inside out. It's a practice of giving oneself to what can be learned or gained through experience and not just ideas of the mind. Once this embodiment takes shape and begins to live within you, the mind often has no choice but to let go and to adapt. You move with, cry with, and laugh with the story and the song of who you walk with.

There is no turning back to what were only ideas.

Because of this walk, I am forever connected to older women, to refugees from Iraq, to the U.S. and Iraq war, the many expressions living within Muslim life and so much more in a way that I would have never imagined. No article, or book, or political leaning would have educated me in this way. I believe in my deepest places, after walking with thousands of people like these women, that the questions, the mysteries, the relationships, and the spaces between what we deem is right and what we deem is wrong are more important than ever.

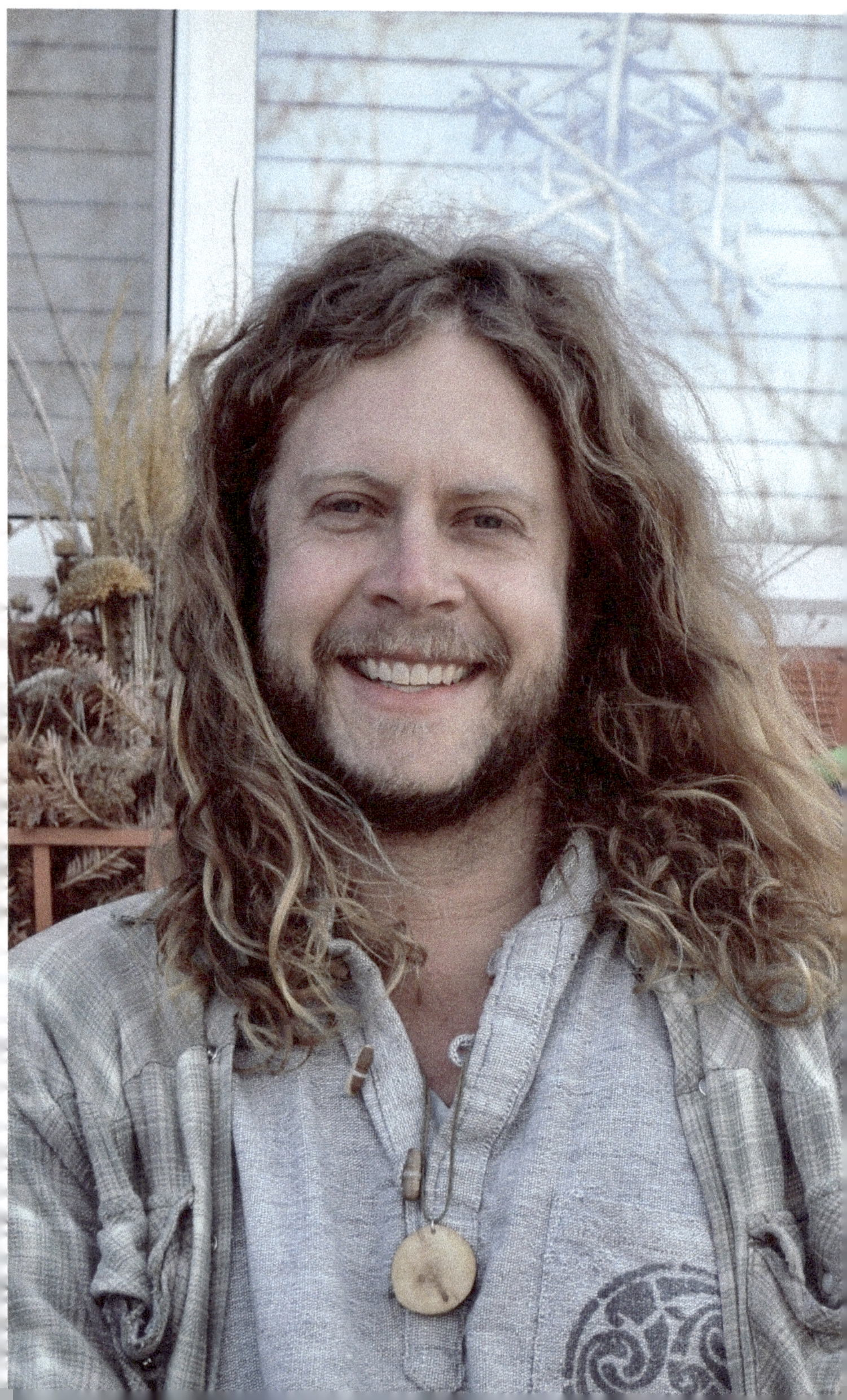

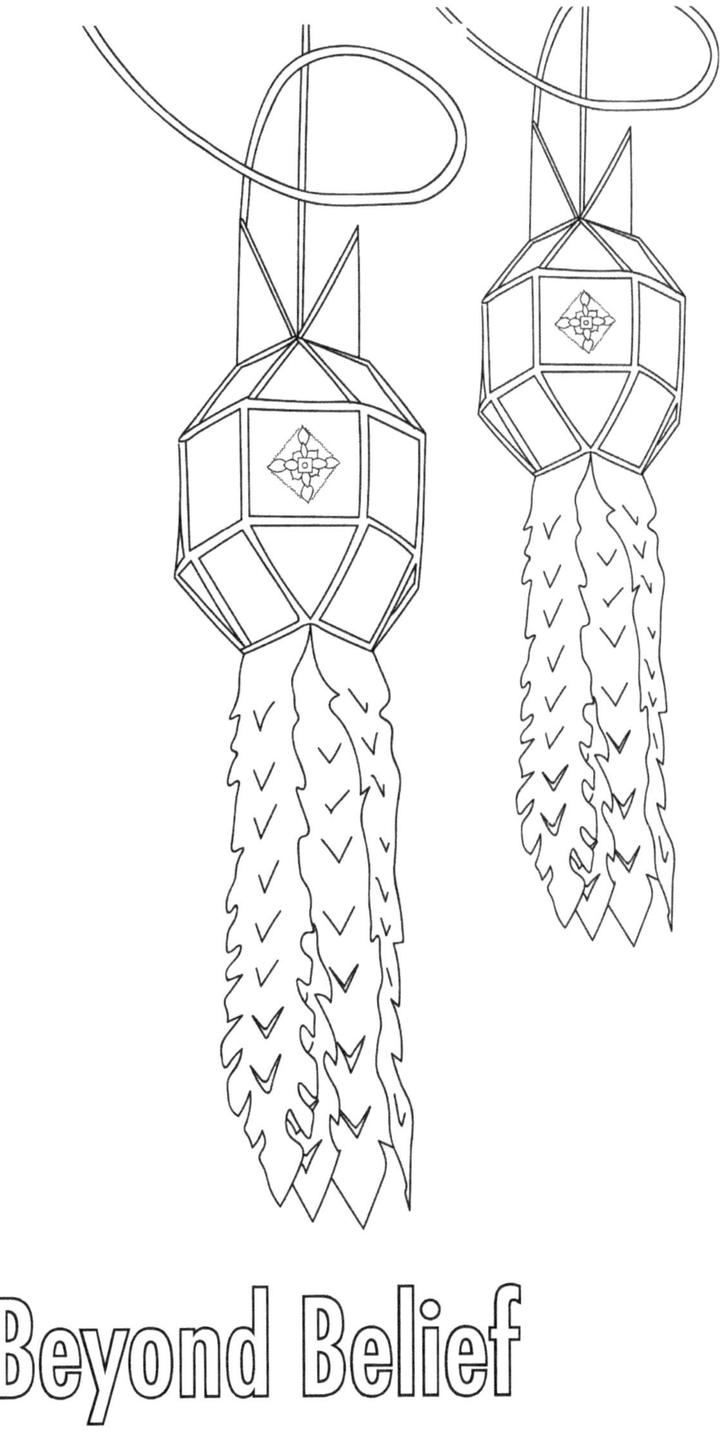

Beyond Belief

Written By: Sloane Kohnstamm

The comfort of my self-confidence was ripped away from me like a blanket from a child. Up until this point in my life, I was unaware that my feeling of self-worth was something that could be stripped from me. As a sophomore at the University of Colorado at Boulder, I was searching for my tribe—people like my home friends who loved me for who I was, and helped me feel strong and passionate about life. In this process, at the age of 19, I found myself living with three fraternity boys, who valued hobbies such as spending many hours at the gym, beer, and objectifying women.

"No matter who I surround myself with," I thought, "my values and sense of self will never be shaken from me." At the beginning of the year these three guys made fun of me for small aspects of who I was, like my love for yoga or for being a vegetarian. As the year progressed, I found myself as the odd one out in discussions such as whether or not we should install a stripper pole in our living room. Although I felt so strongly that my position to oppose this absurd proposal was just, my roommates badgered me until I began to question if I was the one who was being too sensitive, taking things too seriously. The absurdities of living in this household only intensified. (For example, I was the only roommate that opposed the others dumping their cat's shit over the neighbor's fence instead of cleaning out the pan.) With time, I felt weaker in my own body and using my own voice, feeling that I would be judged for expressing anything I didn't agree with. At this same time, my Grandmother Beth was diagnosed with cancer. I felt lost. Unstable. Weak. Helpless.

The opportunity arose for me to study abroad, so I packed my bags and flew to India. I was determined to pursue yoga in the culture that it arose from, and immediately signed up for a Yoga Practice and Theory course. I attended these classes multiple times a week, and began a practice in meditation and mindfulness.

Living in India was quite a change from living in the wealthy, party filled bubble of Boulder, Colorado. Monsoon season meant no power for 12 consecutive hours regularly, and as a woman it was unsafe to leave the hostel after dark. So, I had very little opportunity to avoid my incessant thoughts of not enoughness that my roommates had instilled in me with distractions such as movies or social media. The only foreseeable option for me was to learn to manage my thoughts, and fully embody the practice of meditation.

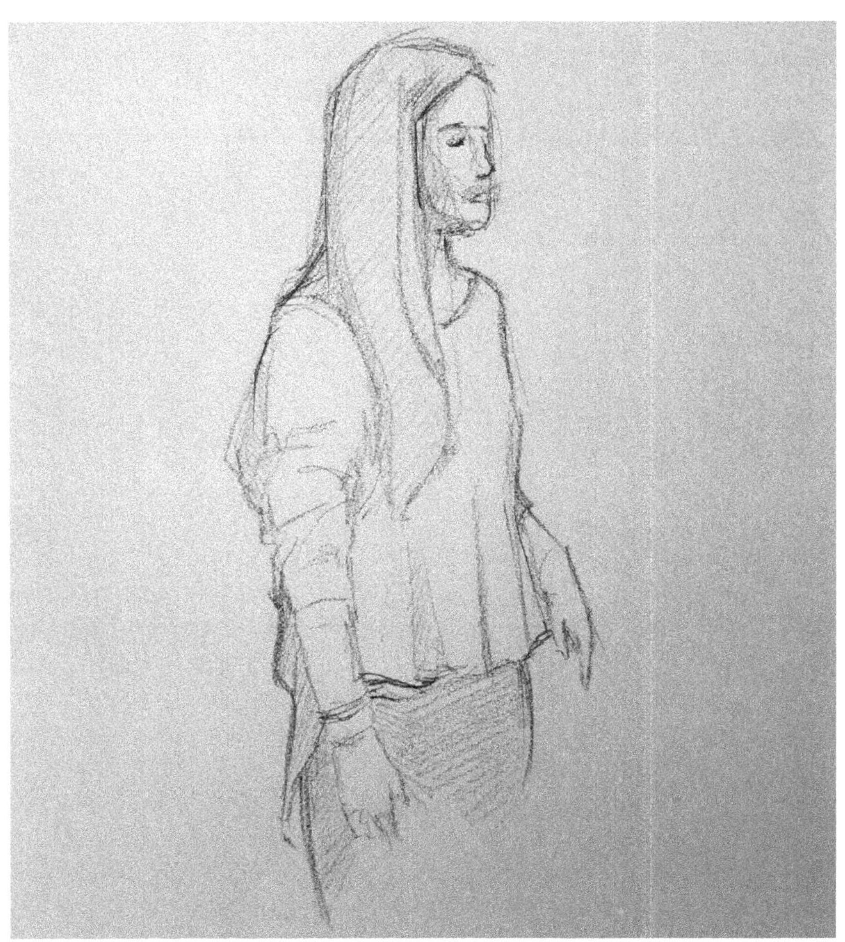

As my practice strengthened, it was as if I could finally hear myself again. As if I had been hearing my roommates' thoughts in my head, and I could finally hear my own voice. Like I had connected with something even bigger than me. Something I had not experienced before. Each day I grew to love myself more and ride the wave of my thoughts—seeing them for what they were—just thoughts.

August 10th of that year was a day I will never forget. It was my 20th birthday, and with the mindset of non-attachment, I attended Yoga Theory and Practice class early in the morning, like any other day. Although I felt little need to announce to anyone that it was my birthday, one student in the class decided that she would take it upon herself to make the announcement.

"Oh Slo-Anne," my warm and maternal yoga teacher said to me calmly. "What is it that you desire on this day?" "Uhm..." I replied hesitantly, "I want to continue to grow as a person?" "No Slo-Anne," she responded quickly, "think deeply." I told her that my Grandmother had cancer and I would love nothing more than to spend quality time with her in the next few years and to see her feel better.

She sat the class down on the floor, and began a meditation and visualization that I was by no means prepared for. "Imagine Slo-Anne with her Grandmother," she said in her soft Indian accent. "Imagine Slo-Anne's Grandmother laughing and smiling." This continued for what felt like an eternity. The energy in the room was penetrable and thick as if it could be cut with a knife. I felt a huge lump in my throat. Before I could even comprehend what was happening, tears started streaming down my face.

A few days later when the power was on and the internet was working, I got a ping in my inbox. It was a letter from my Grandma Beth with the subject line, "Your Birthday!" She explained to me that the strangest thing had happened. She was not feeling well, and was getting progressively more ill. But on the evening of my birthday in Minnesota, which was the morning of my birthday in India, she began to gain strength. I was stunned.

Since that day she grew healthier, and my Grandmother went on to beat cancer.

To this day I cannot explain what happened, or if that was pure coincidence. But on that day, I promised myself then and there that I would never forget the magic that meditation brought. Taking the time to sit every day and trust my own internal compass, and send love to others is something that I cannot describe and something that felt so integral to my being at that point. The experience was something Beyond Beliefs. I felt like I had found myself. I felt whole. Stable. Hopeful. Strong.

So now, 8 years later, do I still remember the promise that I made to myself? To be honest, the last year and a half of my life have been a little rough. I have experienced sexual assault, and it has been challenging to overcome this trauma. Although I have come close to losing my faith both in myself and the Universe, the memory of my experiences in India help me feel a sense of strength. There is an underlying memory of comfort and trust in myself. Something that is important for me to remember as I reflect on this story. It is time for me to muster the strength to invest in myself again. To re-build my faith and ability to

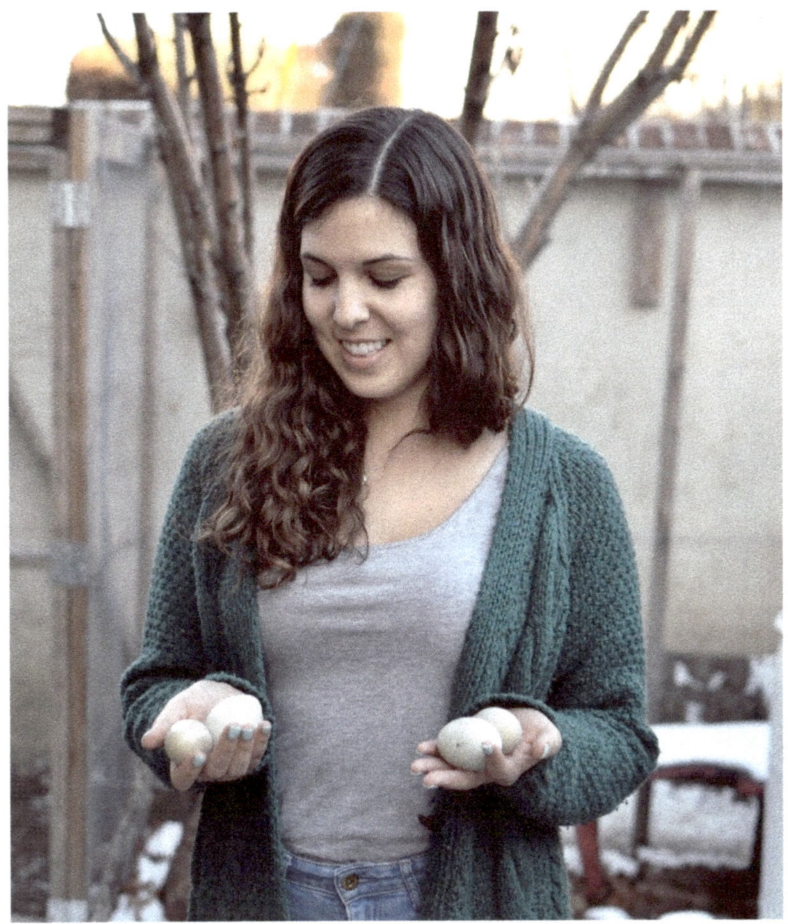

trust.

Although my sweet Grandmother Beth has now passed away, I feel grateful to have her as an Angel looking down on me as I re-commit to this inherent knowing of strength within myself that is Beyond Beliefs.

The Climb

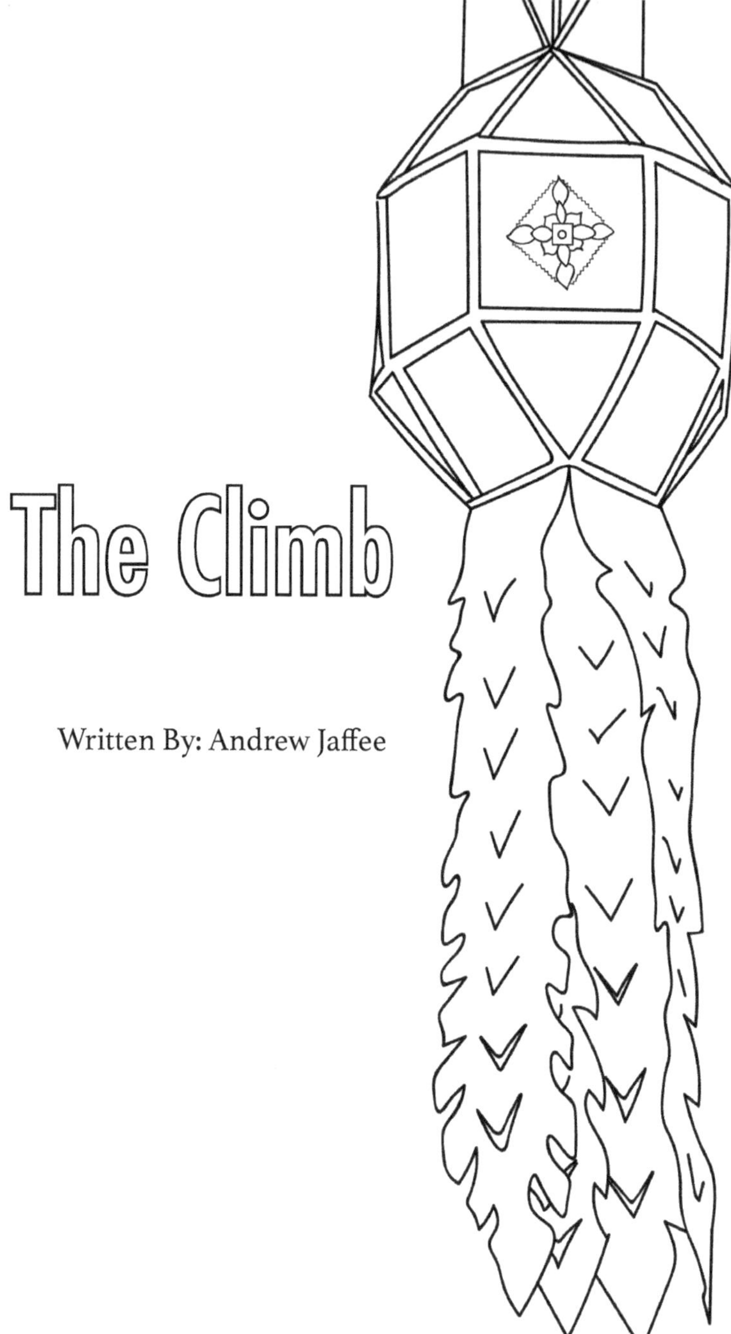

Written By: Andrew Jaffee

I come to you today only with my own personal ponderings. I don't have any answers on what is true in this life. This is simply my own experience.

I completed my first outdoor lead climb at the end of May, 2017. It was the culmination of a year and a half of training. It was a beautiful day out. The sun was setting as I prepared to lead the climb. This would be my first time ever placing the rope instead of top roping on a job that someone else had set. Some holds were hard and I almost fell a few times as I struggled up the face of that mountain. When I reached the top that day, I looked out and saw the last bits of sunlight touching the earth from Golden all the way to Denver. I felt on top of the world. I had worked hard for it. I had practiced in the gym for a long time. My hands were calloused and rough from the work I had put in. Being outdoors, feeling that real rock beneath my hands, smelling the mixture of sweat and earth, I knew I had accomplished something. I remember saying it felt as though this was my second bar mitzvah; I had truly become a man that day. It took me a while to feel brave enough to join the climbing community in Colorado. At first, I was intimidated by the other climbers and the whole culture itself, but when I got on that wall again for the first time, I knew I was meant for it. It felt right, and I was good at it. At the time, this was what strength looked like to me. It was measurable. I could see the progression in each new hold I made and each fall I took.

These were all steps, leading me down a predictable, comprehendible path. I was diagnosed with cancer just a week after that outdoor climb. It was June, 2017. This launched me into truly uncharted territory. It's a battle that I continue to fight, a battle that seems to have enveloped my whole life. Since I was diagnosed, my beliefs have changed significantly. My strength isn't as measurable now. I can't see myself progressing like I used to. Now, it's more of quality over quantity. Being able to climb out of bed is a huge accomplishment for me. Sleeping less than 14 hours a day feels like success. Walking my dog around the block is my new mountain to ascend. Often, I find it is very easy to get down on myself. I don't think I'm doing enough. I could try harder. I'm just being lazy. Sometimes, just giving myself the grace to feel sick and vulnerable is all the strength I can muster for the day.

This new understanding of strength, of how far it actually

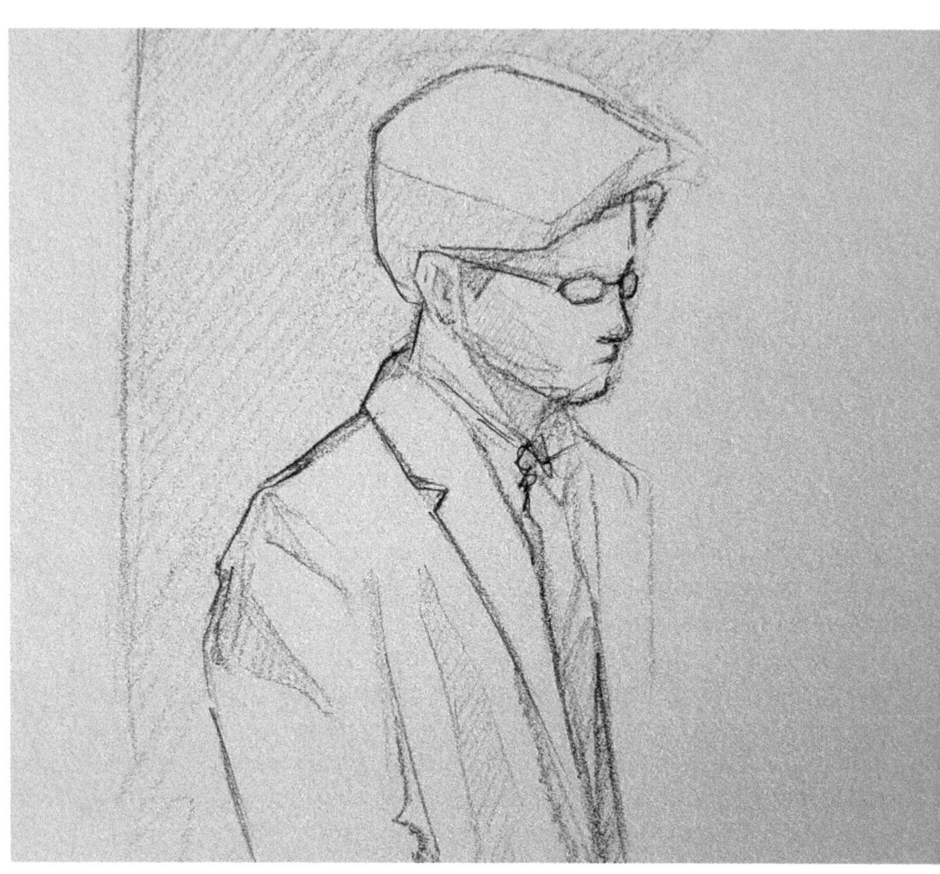

drives a person, has really opened myself to others. It has shown me that every person, at all times of the day, are fighting their own personal battles. It has taught me to be less critical of others. I see now that everyone is struggling in their own ways. No person's struggle is bigger or smaller than another's. Everyone's struggle is valid. It's my wish that people would afford themselves the grace that I give myself in not feeling strong at times.

Before this diagnosis, the mentioning of a miracle seemed trite and uninformed. It was an admission that there was some higher power, the man in the clouds that could dictate my life. I didn't believe in predestination and I wouldn't give credence to anything that even pointed in that direction. Now, I see that there are miracles everywhere around us. This idea all started on an exceptionally bad day in the hospital. My mother, witness to all of my pain, told me of an Albert Einstein quote that she had heard in a meditation recording. It went something like: "There are two ways to live your life. One is as though nothing is a miracle. The other is as though everything is." This struck me hard. I couldn't see there being no miracles in the world with all the good things that were happening to me in this terrible time of my life.

Miracles were all around me just in me opening my eyes every morning. It was a miracle that my GoFundMe was supported enough that I didn't have to go into massive amounts of debt. It was a miracle that my uncle happened to be head of pathology at Brigham and Women's at Harvard. It was a miracle that I have parents and friends and a girlfriend that care enough to help me through each and every new struggle that I face. Once, I was upset that I had to be driven from the hospital to my radiation appointment, just a mere block away, on such a beautiful day. I complained to the man that strapped me into the truck. It turned out that this man wheeling me had beaten lung cancer as a child.

He told me that the world may seem unfair at times, but that yes, things do get better. What else could these good fortunes be if not miracles? Now, while I don't think of myself as more religious, I definitely feel more spiritual and understanding of the flow of the universe. Good and bad things happen to both good and bad people all the time. I feel, though, that giving the good things credence as miracles is a small way to be thankful for what I have rather than feeling as if the universe owes me anything.

Finally, in the long hours and days of lying in bed, I really started to analyze the difference between simply being alive, and truly living. I often don't feel like a survivor, and yet, I still survive. Being bedridden forces me to be present every second of the day. At times I am so immobile that my reality and my dream life intertwine. I spend more and more time asleep because, in my dreams, I am truly free. I can walk without my cane. I can fly without wings. I blend in in a crowd. I am no one's inspiration or motivation, and that feels good. My dreams have limits, though. While I feel so free of the pain of life's limitations, I will be lucidly reminded that I am, in fact, only dreaming and that it is not my time to stay in this dreamland forever. So I wake up.

As I lie in bed all day I remember my past life. Going out with friends. Laughing. Climbing. Adventuring. That was truly living for me. I was an early childhood educator, a life's calling which I only figured out about six years ago. The transition of going from one that took care of others to being the one cared for was difficult, but it's what I needed, and that needs to be alright for now. I may not be climbing mountains yet, but I'll be damned if that climb in May was that last one of my life. I know deep inside that one day, I'll be back on those rock faces again.

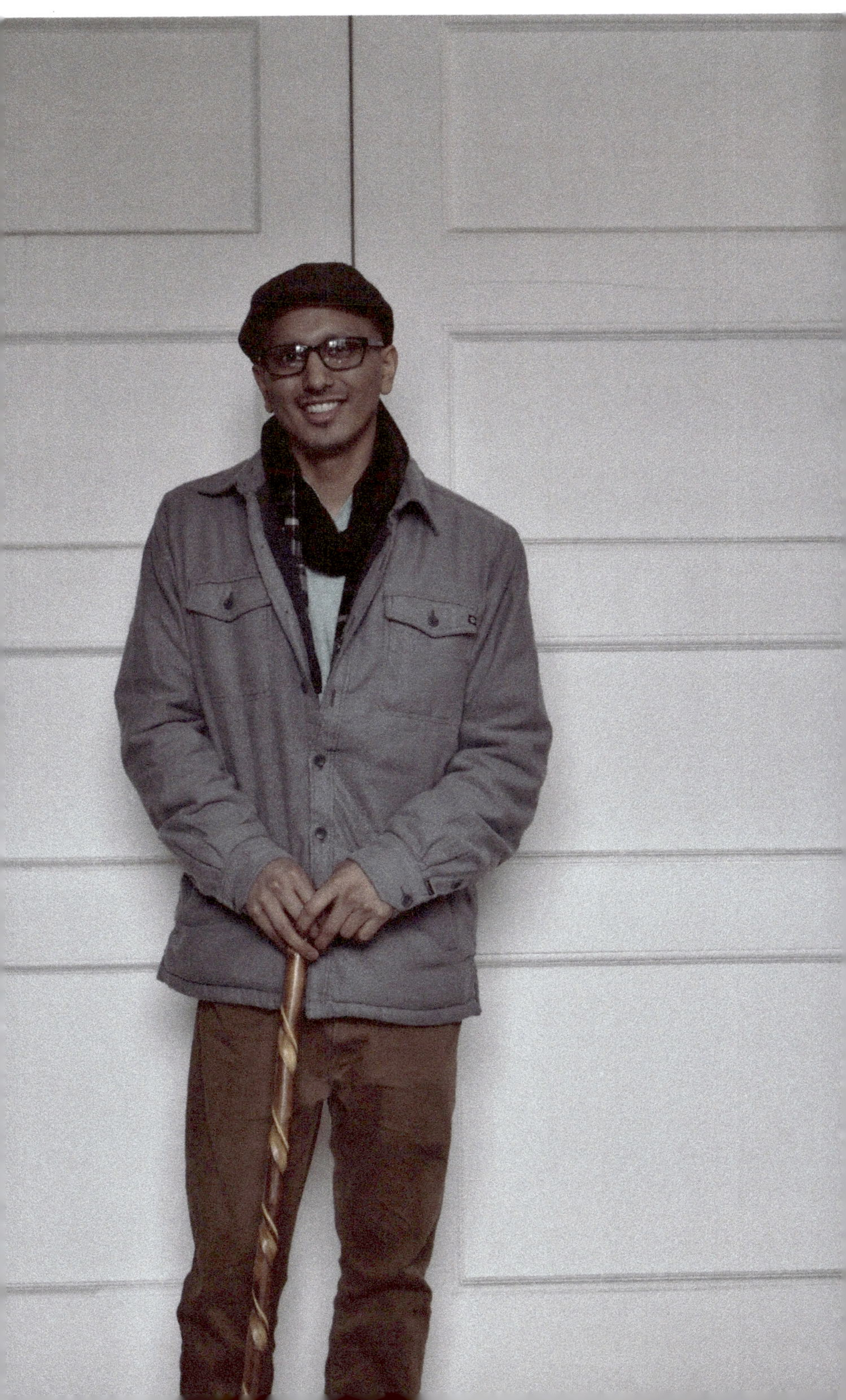

Challenging Steps

Written By: Kriste Peoples

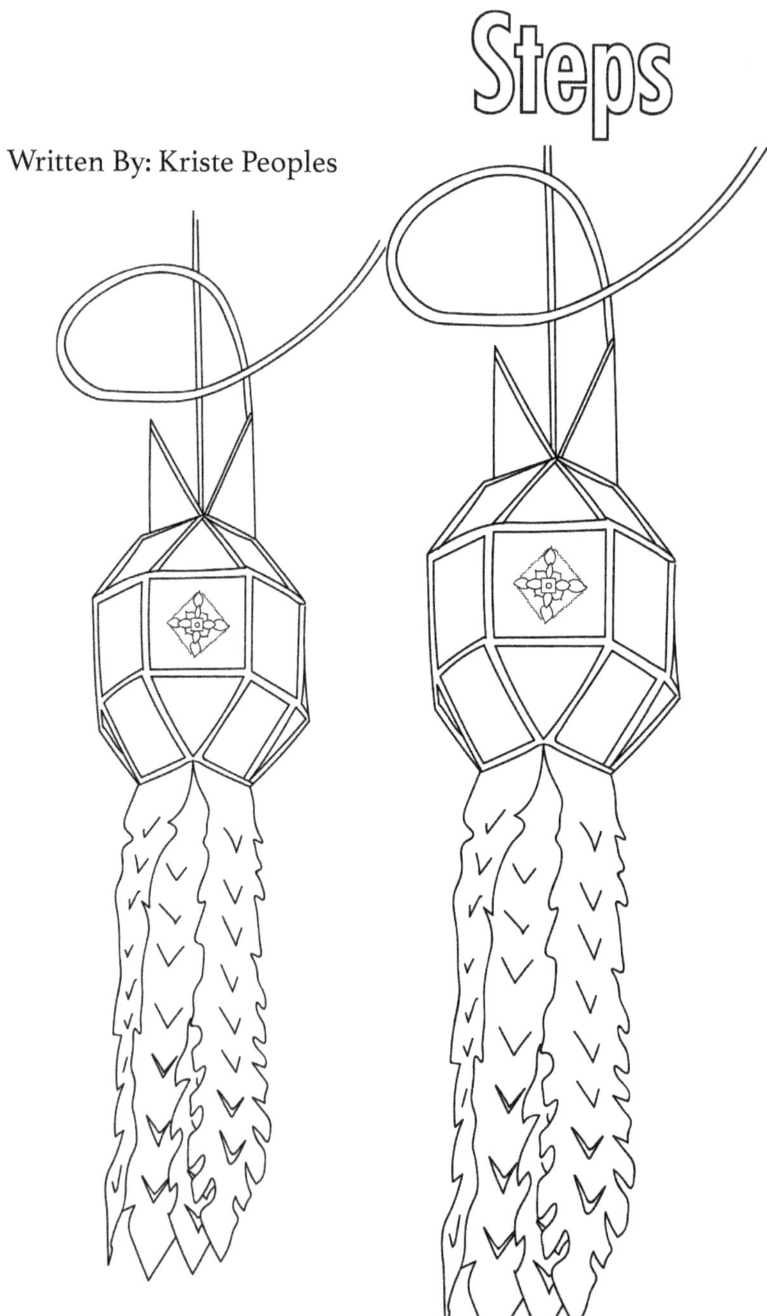

My name is Kriste, and I am a loser. It wasn't always this way, and to understand my story better, I need to take you back to the starting point, which, truth be told, isn't three months ago, or even last year. The most accurate point of origin would put us at the time of Eve—in the garden—when she got her first taste of shame, selfdoubt—and the naked truth.

But I'm short on time, so I'll keep it current.

It was last year, December 28th, and after weeks of walking and hiking and running, we were nearing the end of our monthlong challenge to complete 10,000 steps a day. It was a virtual thing, and our group had been tracking progress in a shared spreadsheet. There were 30 of us, maybe, at the start, then 20 something barely two weeks in and by our last count, no more than 8 real contenders left. Of those 8, I was near the lead.

I'm a women's running coach, and if you knew me at all, you'd know I'm a natural cheerleader. By default, I'm generally helpful and mostly nonthreatening. I am the wind beneath your wings, the wind in your sails, the wind at your back. I have got lots of wind.

So, it's the 28th nearly 10 o'clock at night when I get a note on our Facebook page from Tanya, one of the participants. "Hey, Kriste," it goes, "make sure you log your miles for the past week because, I've noticed you haven't been entering them lately."

So, I go into the spreadsheet and see that next to her, I'm the only one close to winning. Then it hits me—she wasn't offering me an innocent 'friendly' reminder. She was angling to secure the win. Her ambitiousness was naked, shameless—balls. Suddenly, I'd been plunged into a competition I hadn't counted on. It felt aggressive, un-teamly—because weren't we in this together, being each other's cheerleader and wind, liking every stupid post, offering candoity feedback at every perceived slump and setback? This wasn't a cutthroat competition, I wanted no parts of it. Or so I believed. Until Tanya and her bareassed ambition.

A trigger is something that sets off a memory or flashback that transports a person back to the event of her original trauma. Triggers are very personal. Different things trigger different people. The survivor may begin to avoid situations (i.e. cutthroat step challenge competitions) and stimuli that she thinks triggered the flashback. Put another way, Tanya and her friendly ass reminder was pissing me off.

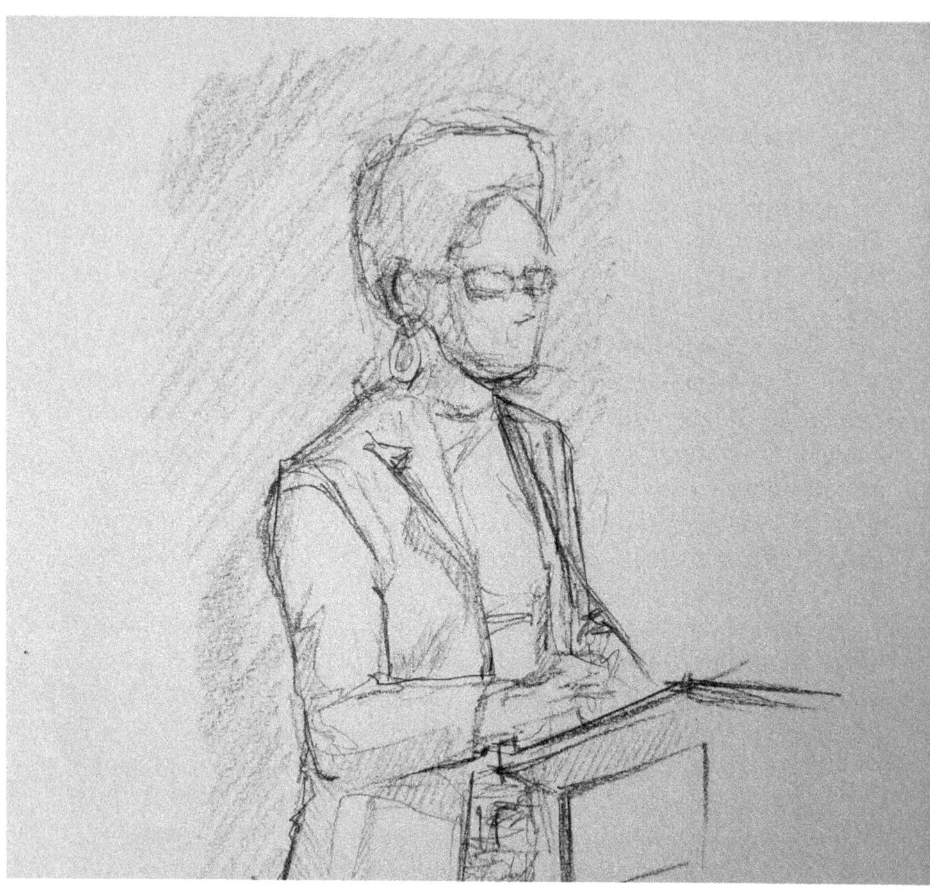

I lay awake running the gamut of emotions that were shooting through me like fire water.

Who is this bitch policing my steps?

I should let her win. She's been on a weight loss journey and this would mean so much to her.

She doesn't care how I'm doing, she just wants to crush me.

I don't even belong in this competition.

Never once had I thought of reasons I should win. Worse yet, it took something as innocuous as a step challenge to show me what a small game I'd been playing with myself for way too long. Her direct hit had knocked my blinders sideways just enough to see my high-road humility had all been bullshit. Why couldn't I want something as openly, as shamelessly as she had? How long had I been backing myself into corners without taking a real chance at first place—or any place? Where had it come from, this look-don't-look self-deprecation, devaluation, and outright, auto-neurotic self-dismissal?

Fuck this shit, I said. I'm going to win.

I threw the covers off and dove into the spreadsheet. By my calculations I needed more than 30,000 steps for the win. If you're following the math, that translates to about 15 miles, and for an ordinary Thursday it meant I'd have to get creative.

That night I looked up a gym with an indoor track, packed a bag of exercise clothes and hung it on the doorknob so I wouldn't miss it on my way to work. I laid an extra set of running clothes across my bed so I'd have fewer excuses in the morning when I tackled my first round of miles.

I called my brother Carl after running the first 7 miles that morning. We'd run a 10k together a few years ago and I made up a game we played in the last mile when he got tired. As a way to stay motivated, we picked out runners to pass and let them be our focus for a few hundred yards at a time.

"What got me," I said, "was you picked people blocks ahead of us, while the ones I spotted were barely an arm's reach away—and I wasn't even tired. You made us work for it," I told him. I told him how I realized I'd been picking safe bets for a long time and that somewhere in me I hadn't believed I deserved to win. I had been afraid.

"Yeah," he said, "and who are you to 'let' her win?" "I know," I said. "It's bullshit, right?"

"Yeah," he said. "You're disrespecting her and the process by cheating."

Sometimes only family can call you out in order to really get it.

I'd go on to walk 3 miles at work then take my crusade to the indoor track for 8 more just to clinch the deal. That's 18,000 more steps—which rounds out to 18 miles in the end. And the other thing: that fucking track took 10 trips around it just to get a mile. That's 80 laps for 18,000 steps, for 18 miles for the win.

The first few laps were easy. Then the monotony of running in circles set in. I told myself every step was stomping out old lies I'd believed that had kept me coming in last, undermining my worth, and abandoning my self. Look at you trying to be smart. 2,162 steps. You still in school? Nobody's gonna want you with too much education. 4,281 steps. You're pretty to be so dark. 6,957 steps. Smile, bitch. 9,167 steps. Why aren't you smiling, Kriste? You're making us nervous. 12,813 steps. You don't seem grateful to be here. 15,458 steps. You're so articulate. 17,981 steps. The challenge had become my cause.

So, what's the takeaway to all this: it wasn't just Tanya's ass that got kicked in the end; I had kicked my own. Because I'd almost forgotten what fierce competition, commitment to myself and to being my own cheeerleader felt like. Now I'm better at owning my ambition and going for the win—even if I lose while I'm at it—because I deserve my shot. Tanya took hers and it helped me take mine. Who knows, maybe me taking mine helps you with yours. Because no one's going to give you the win. False humility and rationalizing won't keep you warm at night, either. It's not just what I believe, it's what I know.

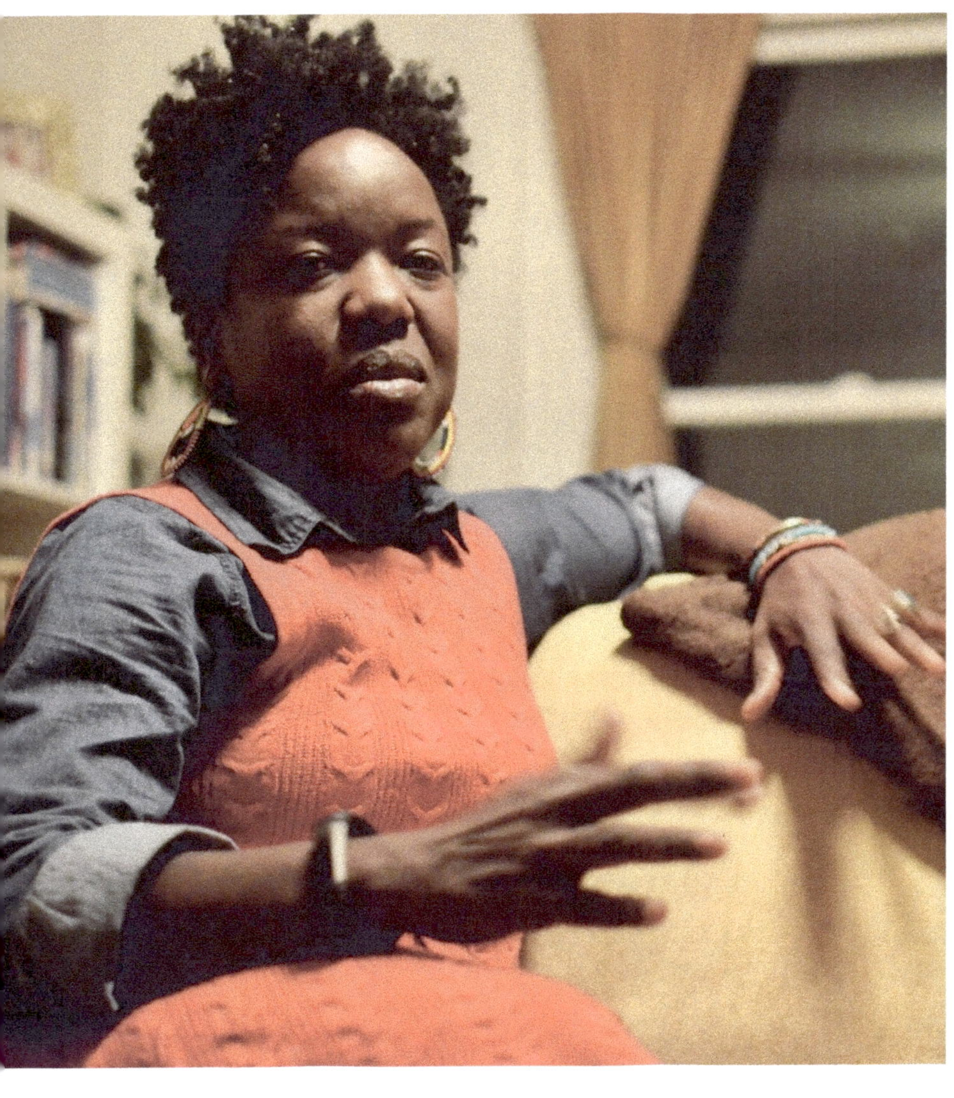

What Do You Want to

"Laughter (possibly).
A feeling of connec-
tion with the room and
hope."

"I'm a visitor, literally just
got off a plane- this was a
rich,
meaningful thing full
of love and community.
What a great glimpse of
this town."

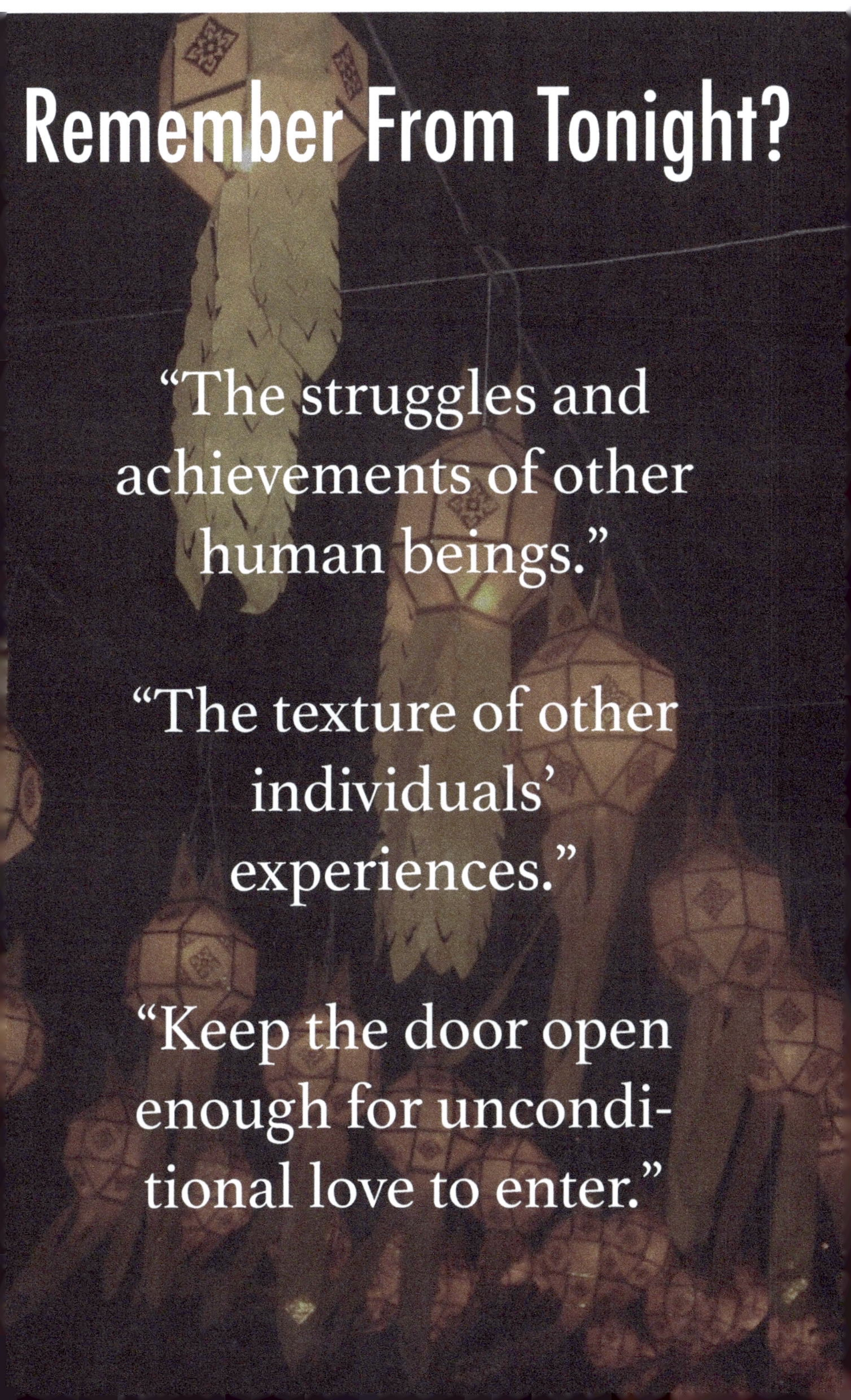

Remember From Tonight?

"The struggles and achievements of other human beings."

"The texture of other individuals' experiences."

"Keep the door open enough for unconditional love to enter."

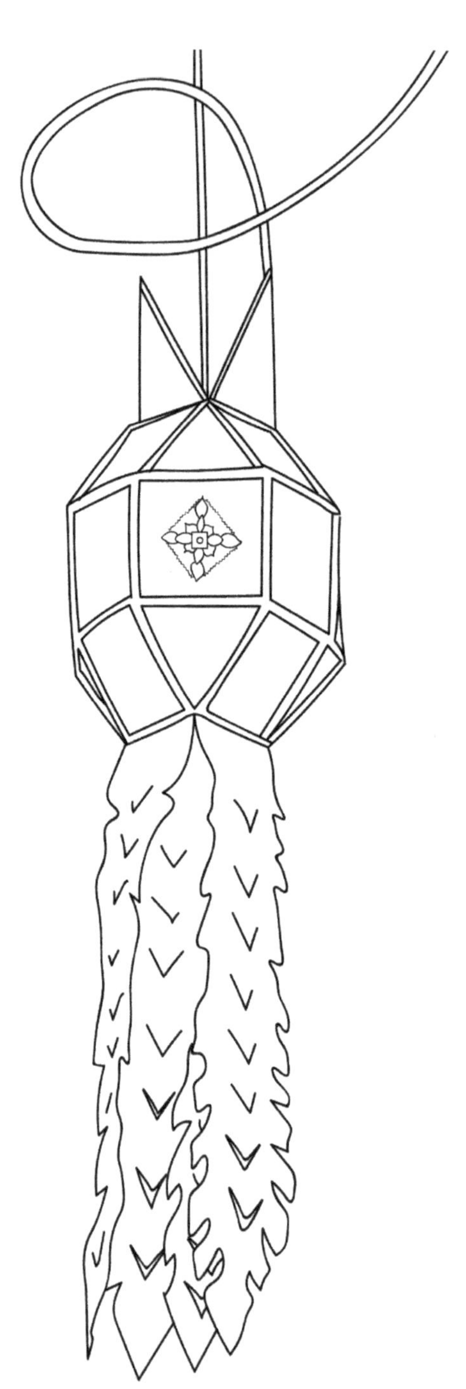

Are You Even A Boy?

Written By: Jarrett Rivera

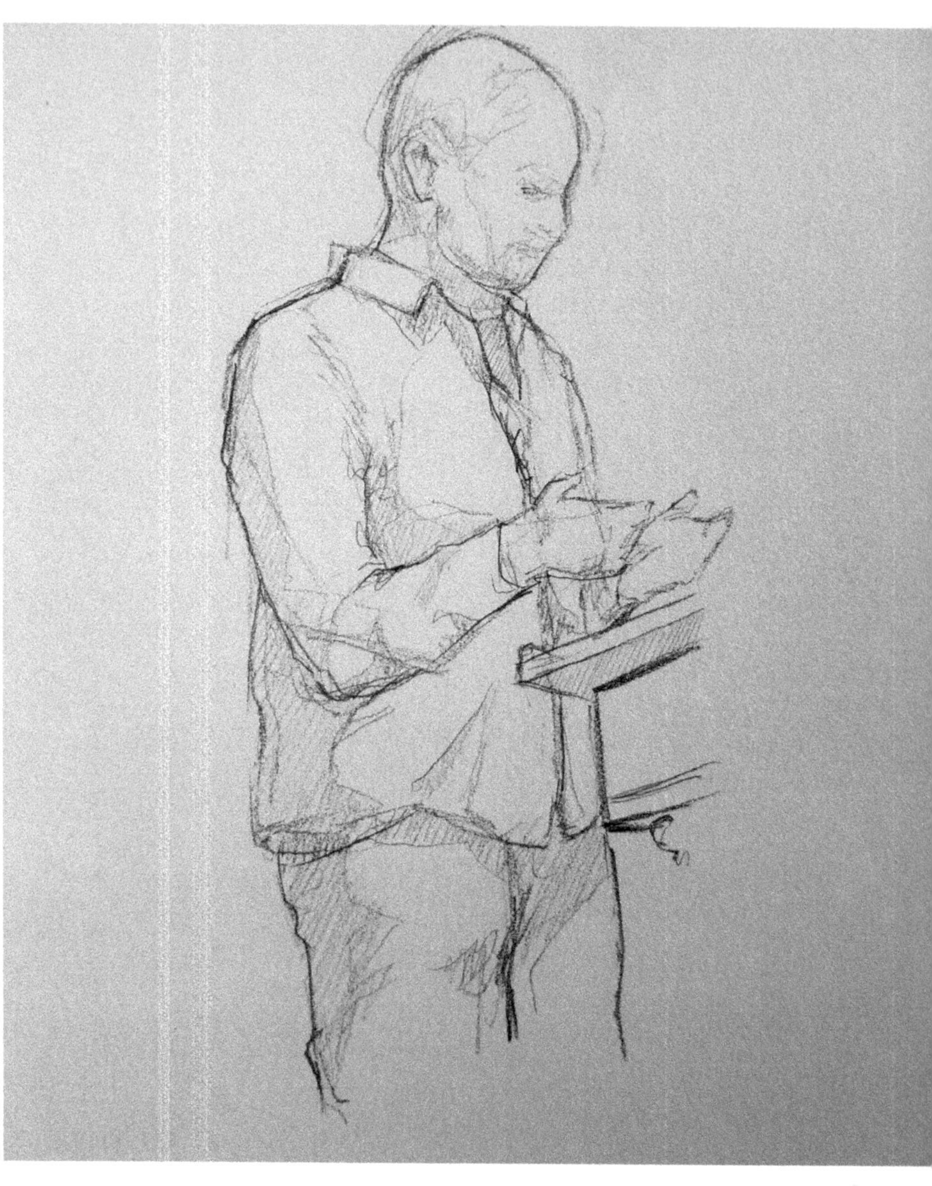

I t's Tuesday night after one of the most stressful, disappointing days of my existence as a grown up, and all I need in this moment is some "self-care" type of pick me up. I had just spent 7 maybe 8 thousand hours studying for this god-awful test, going to class, stress sweating through the exam (probably failing), then running and missing my train to take the bus to go work (arriving late) just to spend the rest of my evening listening to a screaming child call me an asshole and tell me it's my fault he has to live in a children's facility. So yeah! It was a rough day. I decided the only way I was going to want to wake up the next day and, ya know, do it all over again was to glutton down on milk's favorite cookie. I reach into the cupboard and retrieved my already half-eaten package of Oreos and pull out 3 ...5 ...okay 16 cookies, grab a beer stein full of milk and retreat to the couch for a little me time. I dunk my cookie treat into my tall cold glass of milk thinking, "This is it, this is what I've been waiting for –something to finally brighten my day." But, as I pull out my cookie my last hope of happiness breaks in half and plummets into my milk.

And as I sit there watching it sink into that hateful white abyss an actual tear forms on the corner of my eye. I quickly wipe it away as I was trained to do. And it was as if he was standing right there...I heard him. I hear his voice say, "What's wrong with you?" And I'm transported back.

"Oh no no no no. Why? How can I let this happen? Oh god please help me. Please don't let him see. What do I do? What do I do?" I try so hard not to cry as I walk my bike into the garage. The stupid bike chain had fallen off and I knew I wasn't going to be able to fix it. I'm not good at fixing things like my brother. I don't why. I turn the bike upside down and frantically start to reassemble the chain. "Why can't I do this? You're stupid! Stupid!" I squeeze my eyes shut and start to pray out loud. "Please god. Please don't let him come outside. Please please. Please don't let him..."

The door to the garage opens.

I quickly wipe my face. "Have you been crying," my father demands. "No sir," I assert. "What's the matter with you, huh? What'd you do to your bike?" "I don't know, sir. It just fell off." He walks toward me and I automatically begin wincing and cowering. He hits me upside the head expecting me not to flinch from the sharp pain. "It's just the bike chain, moron. Put it back on." I stare at the bike knowing I won't be able to get it on and feeling so scared about what will happen when I can't. I say to him, "I don't think I can get it on." "Hijo de la chingada! What is wrong with you? Are you even a boy? Do you do you have a dick between your legs? Fix the fucking bike!" I no longer am able control my tears.

He's right. Why can't I do this? Why can't I be a man like my brother? I reach for the chain and I desperately try to figure it out. After a moment of watching his useless, pathetic excuse for a son fumbling with a bike chain, my dad slaps me and says "Stop crying, you fucking fairy. Go inside and wait for me. Useless little faggot."

I walk inside trembling from the terror of the impending punishment I would soon undergo. But even more than that, I felt ashamed. If I was a man like I was supposed to be, then this would not have happened. While I waited for my dad to come "set me straight," I prayed to God demanding why I was like this. Why did you make me this way? Why am I so broken?

I return to the present.

Growing up feminine in a strict-Christian, hyper-masculine, Latino household was... grim. My father needed his sons to be men. He needed us to play soccer, go fishing, fix cars, and (insert other stereotypical masculine activity). And my brother was just that. Perfect in my dad's eyes. I was more inclined to play dress up and sing Barbra Streisand showstoppers, or recite Sally Field's "I wanna know why" monologue from Steel Magnolias (powerful stuff, by the way). My dad would have none of my "girlish" antics in his house. He encouraged his friends and my brother to chastise me when I spoke. "You sound like a girl, Maricón," my father would shout. "Be a man!" At a very young age, I learned to keep silent. I hated myself and constantly wondered why I couldn't just be a "normal" boy.

I grit my teeth and clench my eyes and clamor to hear that different voice inside my head, the voice that says, "You don't have to feel this way anymore. You are not useless. You don't need to hate yourself for being gay. You are worthy of love. You are a man. There is nothing wrong with you." My husband walks over to me and gently kisses me on the forehead. He knows I've had a hard day and knows how deep in my head I must be. He recognizes it, even without me saying anything. He grabs the "milk stein" out of my hands and pulls me up to him. He pulls me in so tight like only he knows how to do and gently whispers in my ear, "I love you. You know you've got this." I allow myself to cry on his shoulders as he holds me. I give him a kiss and walk over to the bathroom to splash some water on my face. I look up in the mirror and I like what I see. A full-grown, 30-year-old man with all the sass and femininity I've always had and wished I could have loved for all of these years. I smile and feel the goddess inside me. She's my protector, my warrior, my inner voice telling me to be who I am and I don't have to explain her to anyone. I just know she's the source of all my power. I take a deep breath, spin around, and sashay my ass to bed.

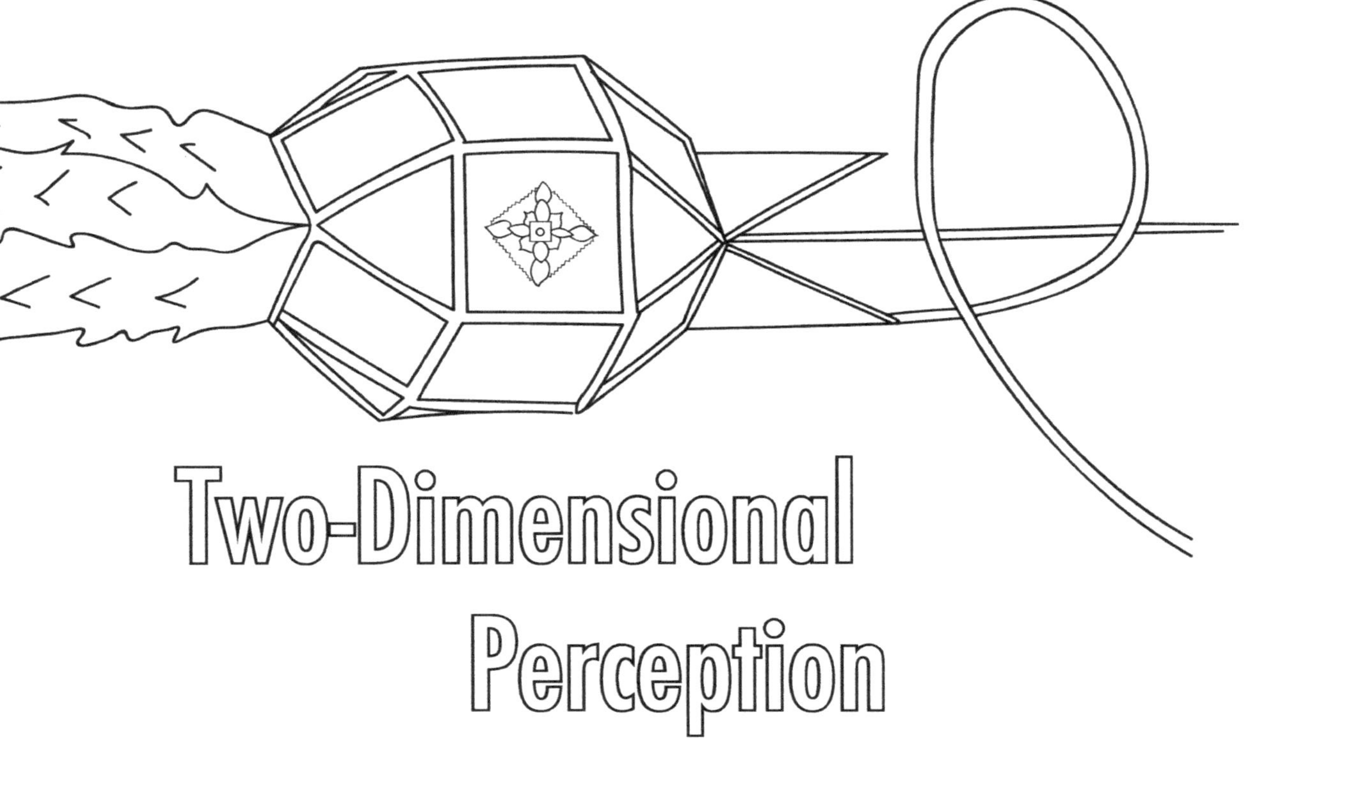

Two-Dimensional Perception

I am here to tell you the truth that other people are too afraid to face. That we have all been lied to about the very nature of our reality. The truth is that the world is flat...

I don't actually believe that the world is flat, but it is something that I deal with in my line of work. For those of you that haven't seen the memes or heard about this: yes, people actually believe this. The idea that the world is flat is shockingly growing in popularity. It's a thing.

I work at a science museum. I teach people that earth carries all of its own history within it, through layers of rock under our feet.

To flat earthers, as they call themselves, I am the enemy that perpetuates the lies of the government.

This is the story of the first moment that I was confronted by a flat earther at the science museum.

I was performing a presentation about space to about 30 members of the general public, and a man raised his hand, pushed his way to the front, and aggressively asked a question "if the world is round, then how do you explain that we can see ships in the ocean at such far distances?!"

I stood there, stunned. In that moment, I felt many layers of emotion at once.

I could sense the atmosphere of the guests in the room. Everyone looked either confused, intimidated, or angry. It felt clear that the entire room was uncomfortable. It was tense. They looked at him, then back at me, then back at him. It felt like a stand off.

On my surface layer, I was perplexed and fascinated: Was he actually insinuating that the world was flat? What is wrong with him?

Below the confusion, I felt a churning mantle of emotion. The flat earther came at me all angry and insulting, and I had an instinctive feeling that I had done something wrong.

This feeling comes from my own internalized sexism that started in my childhood. Growing up in my family, I learned that as a female, my role is to support men, to please them, and to make

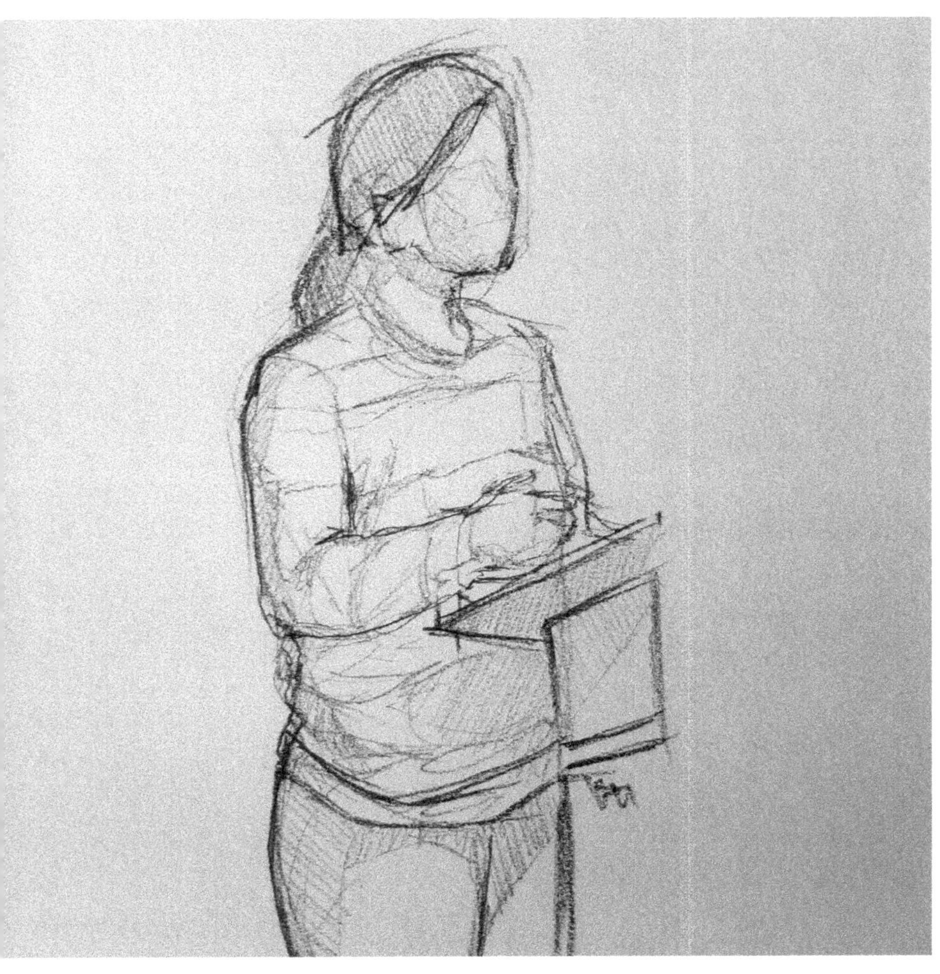

them feel good about themselves. Women served the men, If a man told me that I was wrong, it was because I was wrong.

It happens in the museum. Men who don't know anything about space tell me that im wrong.

The first dozen times it happened, even when it's over something as absurd as the shape of the planet, I still have that moment of pause, of uncertainty. If a man tells me that I'm wrong, then I'm wrong and I'm sorry.

In that instant, I felt that piece of that insecurity from that old story take its final, gasping breath, and fizzle out. I realized that I could not be intimidated. I know something here and it needed to be shared. Step into your power. Speak up.

Deeper in the core of my being, I was reminded of memories of my mother. Flashback to growing up, my mother taught me that unconditional love was the most powerful force in the universe. She got pregnant in high school and never had the chance to become scientifically literate herself, but she trained me to be a loving person, not to judge people but to try to understand them. She was my cheerleader, my hero, and my best friend. I loved her so much.

Five years ago, my mother became very mentally unwell and everything changed drastically. For years, I reached for her as she spiraled into hallucinations and paranoia, I watched her slip farther and farther away from herself, from her family, and from reality. She thought that the government was trying have her killed and that there were parasites crawling out of her brain. She would act out in public and people would laugh at her and call her crazy. I became her emotional bodyguard.

I was convicted: You will not laugh at my mother. You don't know her like I know her. You don't know what a beautiful, wise, and loving person she was.

A few months before the stand off with the flat earther at the museum, mom manically informed me that the world was flat. It was the moment I lost hope. I was overcome with a contrast between feeling angry and ashamed of her, and feeling deep sorrow that after years of grappling, my mother had slipped away from me for good. I had lost her.

Back at the museum, facing the flat earther, the tension in the air... To him, I was still the enemy. To all the other people in the room, he was the enemy.

This man standing in front of me at the museum probably had no inkling that I wanted to protect him.

That I wanted so badly to walk with him through an explanation that would make sense and put him at peace, in a space where he wouldn't be mocked or criticized.

I took a breath and began to respond.

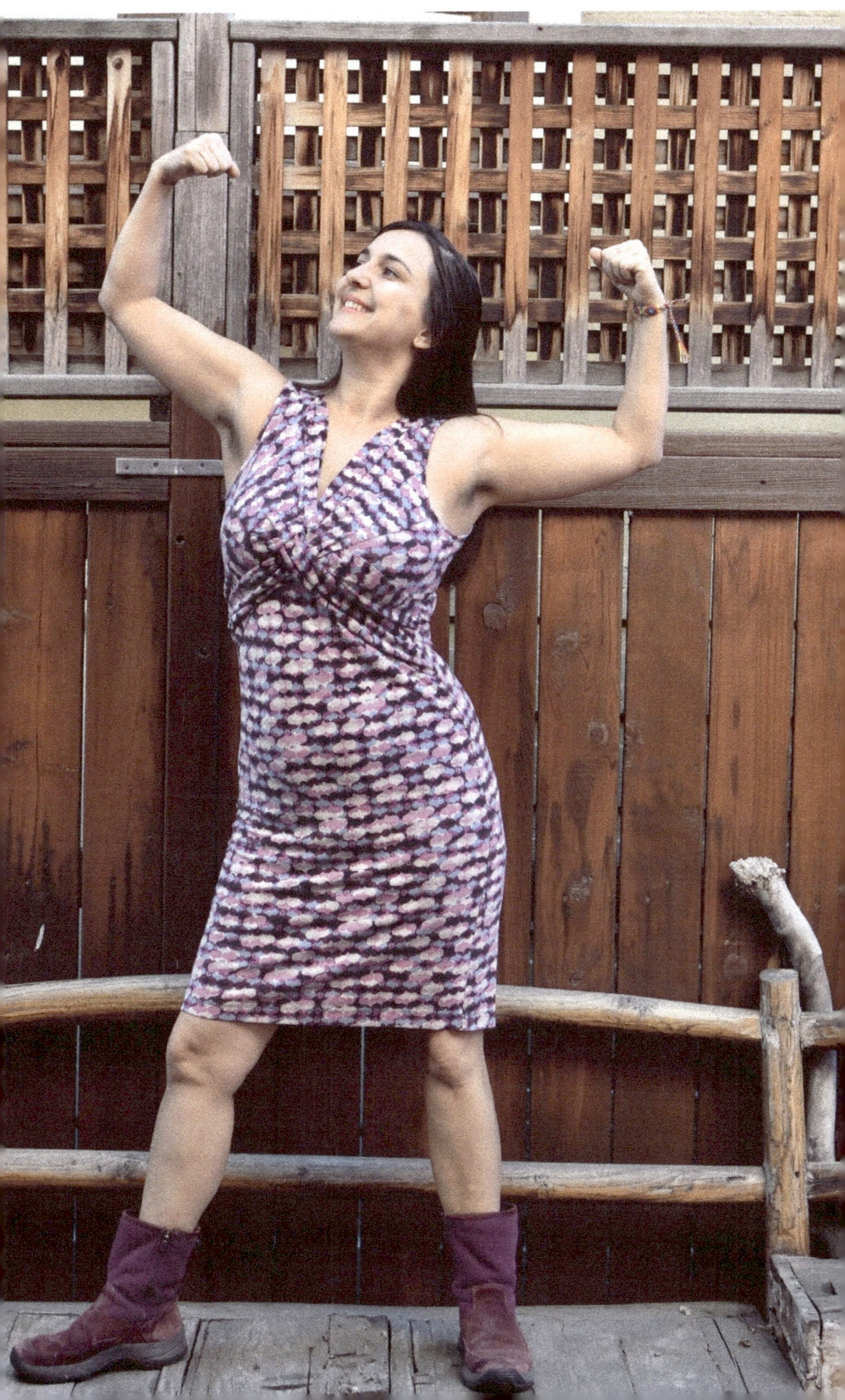

The man cut me off with a comment like, "That's what I thought!" and stomped off.

As this man walked away, he left a vacuum in his place. I had lost him.

In his vacancy, I became committed to always leave the door open for people I disagree with, no matter how wrong they are. So that one day he might be ready to come back and talk.

If he can just have one positive conversation with someone at the museum, he might walk away thinking, "well, the entire museum is a conspiracy, except that one person that I spoke to...I want to talk to them again."

As for my mom, right now, my mom is missing. I wish I knew where she was. She is somewhere on the streets of the USA or Mexico. I imagine she is all alone and people are scoffing at her as she rants to herself. I try to accept this. So, If you see my mom out there in the world, please just...don't lash out at her. Leave the door open a crack. Maybe even give her some love on my behalf.

In this country, we seem to be at a liminal point; splitting into two different realities. We are
turning each other into enemies. And the only way to get back on the same page with each other is if we can keep the light on for our enemies, in case they can ever find their way back home.

As she became more and more aggressive and manic, I have found the irony in it. It was as if this was all part of her plan, that she was preparing me for this my entire life. She taught me love and acceptance as a kid, then she pulled a 180 and became so difficult to love and accept. This has made her my greatest teacher.

What Do You

"Find your own truths. They are uniquely yours and they will set you free. Find them, claim them, celebrate them."

"Everything happens for a reason, but not every reason needs to make sense."

"I believe in finding gratitude in the moment- being in the moment- when I can see something in the word around me that offers reflection or learning to help me continue moving forward on my journey."

"I believe that people can and will always surprise you."

"The power and necessity of storytelling. Of sharing in order to understand."

Believe In?

"I have spiritual beliefs, but don't really believe in anything specific. Sometimes I feel like I don't believe in anything but then I try to believe in people more, though it's hard."

"I believe in God. I believe in people. I believe in science. As well as magic and miracles. We all make mistakes and have our victories. It's just a half a glass of water, never half full or half empty."

"#1 My own capacity.
#2 My mom could beat your mom up.
#3 Everyone's an asshole.
#4 Children are soon-to-be assholes."

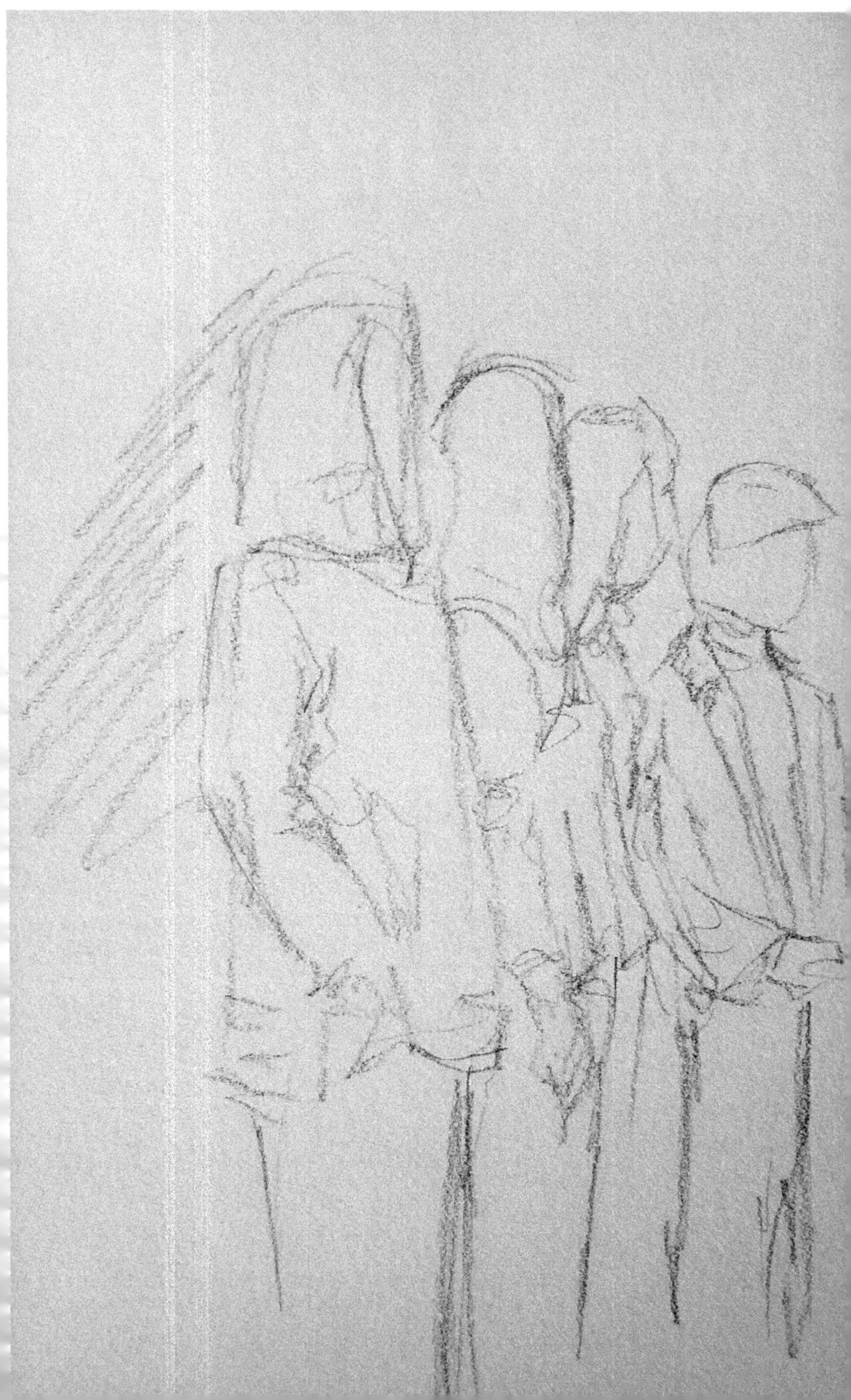

Gravity

Written By: Noah Kaplan

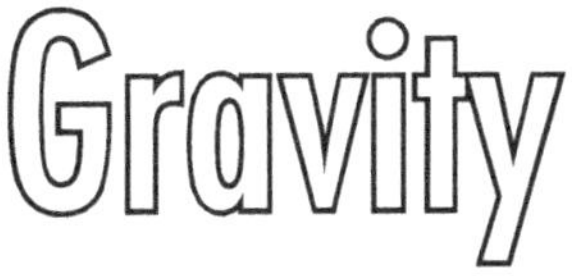

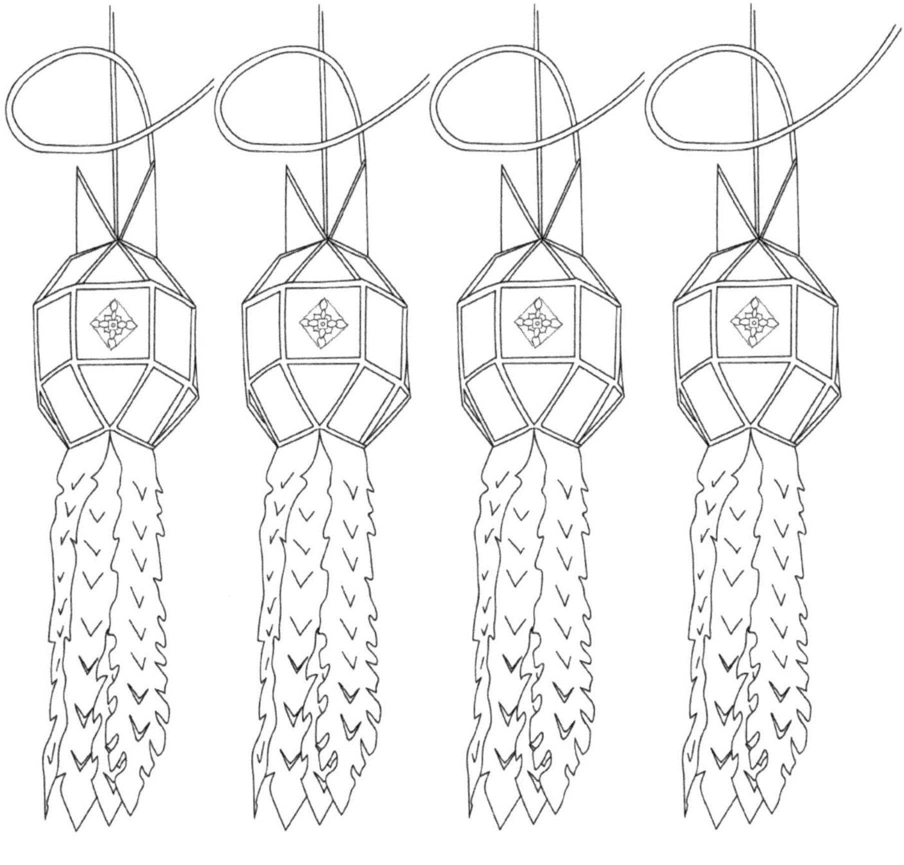

I love to rock climb and I even, kind of, can. I mean I know how to. I know what knots you need and when you need them, I know how to place gear, to build anchors, I know what to do if the rope gets stuck or if the rope's too short. I can envision from the ground where I will go, how I should move, I know what good gear is and I seem to usually know enough to be a little scared.

A few summers I worked as a climbing guide and instructor at a Jewish adventure summer camp in the Rockies and before the summer begins each year I would spend the month leading up to the start of camp with the other guides, scouting

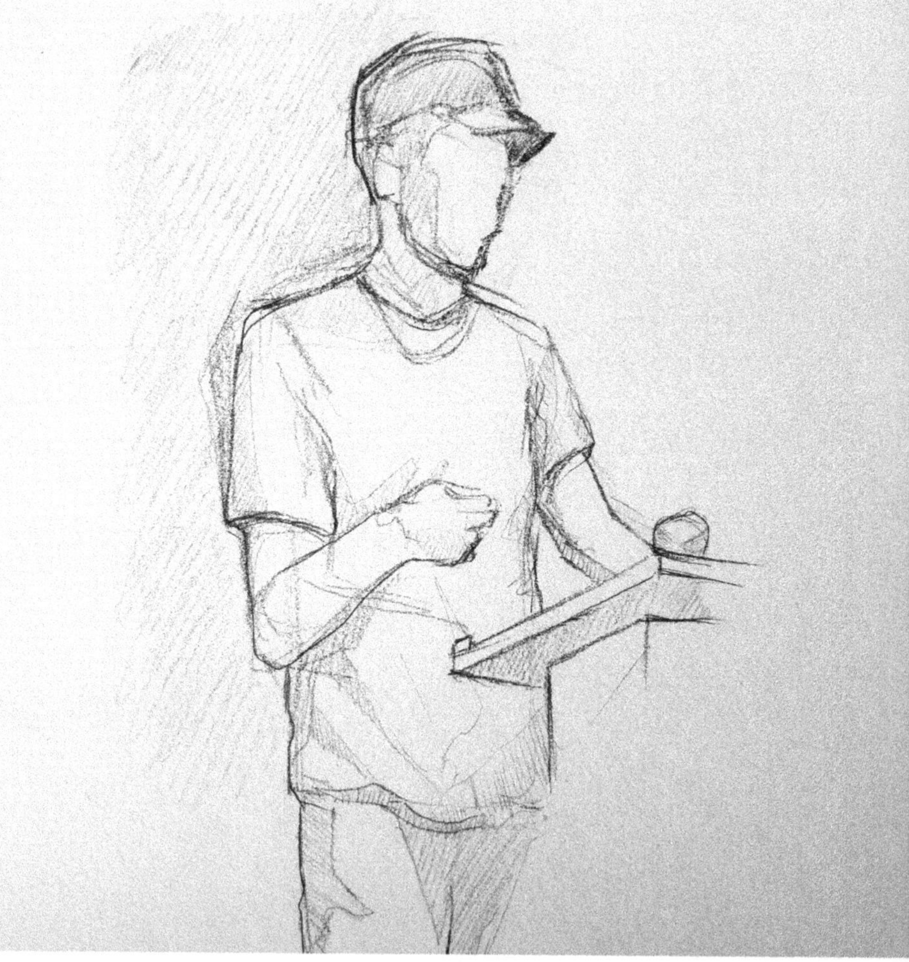

trips to take with the kids, learning to trust one another, watching sunsets and huddling around fires, bunkered in tents during rain storms.

Moti, a dark haired rock animal was our leader, an Israeli hard man with an unquenchable thirst for rock climbing. Leah a lovely spook child from Alaska, tragedy awake, with a coolly competent and contemplative demeanor, an eye for awe, and sensitive skin. Yoniv was our sweatheart, a square jawed irreverent Israeli, all that is loud and playful, always dancing and singing, a puppy dog made of stone and light. And me.

We had come to Devil's head in the Rampart Range of the South Platte, a high forest of rusty rocks, a granite playground crisscrossed by winding dirt bike paths and wandering trails through an aged coniferous forest.

South Platte rock climbing is steep, old school hard, often runout routes on long slabs or blocks of large overhanging granite, tight corners that give you access to roofs that clear to lower angles.

I had felt good that day. I set up a corner, 11c/d, (not too hard but not too soft) which follows a jagged, blocky hand crack to a roof out right.

Right at my pay grade. Something that is quite possible for me, but mostly, my potential uncertain. But I keep moving, scraping my body clumsily, and only slightly panicked up the strange open book. I feel good. It feels good to be there, moving the way I am. Challenged but never shut down, obstacle after cleared obstacle, objective after objective, cleared in a clear way, each move finite and forever, each moment won or lost. It is what it should feel like, to me, this dance with possibility, this holding of the ocean at bay. To find some freedom in my human cage, to push space, to put one hand into the sky after another, to crawl in this barren place, to feel the full tilt of the earth, to consider my limitations and to scrape and scream them back, you either do or you don't—you climb or you fall.

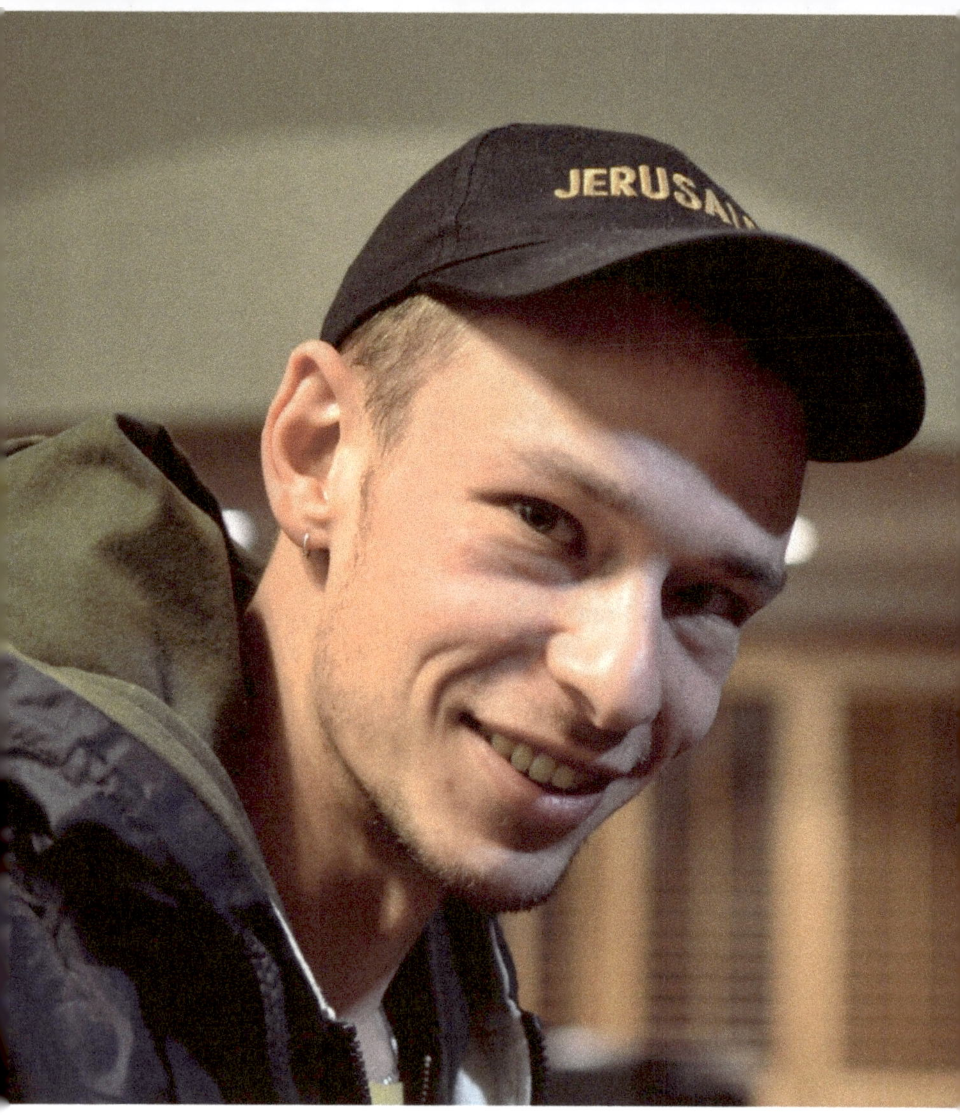

What you believe will in the end determine what will happen to you. Your mind will often be your limitation, before body. You will become what you believe matters most. Dream each moment's potential in time and execute, do not fear the fall, stay centered, loose and tight, when all is telling you you can't, or even that you shouldn't, that there will be some unfortunate consequence to your meager efforts—how easy it would be to fall, to fail.

I am a high school teacher, by trade. When I started

teaching, my preferences told me teaching was an art farming epiphanies, the ah ha summit. But it is less obvious than all that. More messy than all that, but more human, more true as we are. Climbing as I have is a sure privilege, to have had the time to train, to have been shown nature (no longer are we born there, we have to be shown), the preference to put oneself in danger with hundreds, sometimes thousands of dollars of equipment hanging from your waist, like nothing matters, is a certain gift. We are climbing barefoot in this class, with little at our waist, on the rocky lives of one another, the cracks, the imperfections we find to hold on to, to stand on, the rests they offer (how easy it would be to do nothing). They shift every day as we test what is possible, holds break, we stumble, say can't, as we try to recognize opportunity and take it. This is all that is beautiful and broken and scuffed, and impossible in the human story. A 16 year old with bruises on her neck, a 14 year old with grey hair. Esther who draws pictures with me lonely at lunch. Angry boys unwilling to sit, rooms full of no and yes. Won and lost lotteries. Do more, say more, scratch more, think—can I use the bathroom? Can I get a drink?

And what I try and teach my students, if I were to say it, is to realize how much you can hear, how much can you see if you focus.

What comes out of the rocks of the world, and where you can go if you find them. That every opportunity is yours to be made, every room is the room that could change your life. What to do with the pages and screens offered you, what can you see if you look, how high can you climb if you trust yourself, if you jump in time, in this baking classroom, and seize. The closer I look at them, the more I see. I point, I yell, I whisper and crouch, I sit on the floor, I go back and forth, I try and tell them to try, and rarely do I discipline. I guess I leave it to gravity.

I may not belong here. I might be some kind of imposter, some charlatan. A lost clown, out of place, wandering the woods,

telling the wrong jokes to the wrong people and trees, exasperated, nervous. A teacher should have confidence, an objective they believe in, that a child might name or hold onto. My administrators tell me the students must know at the beginning of class what they should leave the class knowing.
Somehow, this seems strange.

Back in the South Platte, clinging to a granite wall, I clear the roof and make the last few moves to gain the upper slab, a period of easier climbing before the finish. I am now 70 feet off the ground, sweating, breathing heavily, bleeding in small places. Alive and happy and conquering. I look down at my rope and notice that the thing has gone untied.

At school, I see her in my class, back for the first time in a week, and she wasn't the bruises on her neck, though we couldn't help but wonder about them now. I was new so I didn't do what I may have done had I known more. I just saw them and like that she was gone, coloring outside the lines in my memory. Looking back, we (and I mean "I") always hoped it was love that had made the bruises. Eager lips put to work by the clumsy passion of adolescence still unaware that it can break things and bring blood to surface. But the bruises were far too dark, far too large to have been made with amour in mind. As I wake up in the dark before my alarm in this cold sweat I know there could not have been tenderness in them, just whoever had failed towards abuse because it's easier to be hard then it is to be soft in this world.

I have seen rock climbing accidents. They aren't pretty. Climbers having broken their legs, their backs. Gravity is indifferent to you. It is not hard to die from a fall. People die from falling all the time. Bikes, down stairs, over cliffs.

I asked Jahlil to talk with me in the hall. He looked at me and rolled his eyes into the back of his head so that all I could see were the icy whites and they trembled—defiance— pure and clear and white hot. He was not impressed by my earnestness either. I could not help him. Because I was me and he was him and that was just how it was and still is.

I believe that a fall from that height would have killed me. I believe that there wasn't much reason I didn't fall, got tired that late in the day, tried to rest, sat back on a rope that wouldn't have been there, and the thing would have slid right through me and we both would have fallen seamlessly to the ground, in an instant, bouncing once on the corner and down again.

Then Johnathon who died in his sleep. We put a rose on his desk and wrote letters to his mom. I played Dixieland jazz as we colored and some of the children cried, and others didn't and I remembered he liked the library because it was quiet and walked with his shoulders and had denied my tomato soup. Mireya, who said that this class made her tired and I turned to her and said me too. And Elijah who was living in a hotel with his mom and couldn't be there, who said to me that high school was hard and how nobody looked at you. Amber who preferred her mother in the custody battle with her abusive father, but Mom might lose it, addicted and fraught as she was. She draws a unicorn and she hugs me awkwardly on her way out the room and then I am alone for a moment. And then I am not.

Ask yourself: What does the rock offer you? Be thankful for tiny imperfections carved out by time, corners to pull and cracks in the wall to shove hands and feet in. This might hurt but you will be stronger for it. It is a sparse environment, akin to a night sky, there are few friends, but remember the longer you look, the more stars appear. What you have is your body and everything else. Keep your feet high. Make sure that you're doing more pushing with your legs than pulling with your arms. Conserve your energy. You have to focus, find your center, tilt it, do your slow, breathy dance with gravity. Keep breathing. When your leg starts to shake or your mind wander, when the fear creeps in or your hands feel sweaty keep moving up, keep doing what needs to be done, keep breathing (remind yourself of this forgotten reflex), remember the important things, the only way to make it work. Stay present, stay calm.

Victor Chen

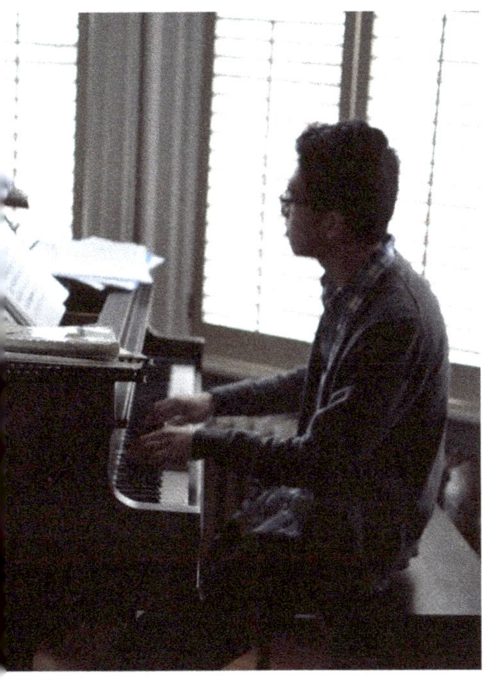

Victor Chen is a local jazz musician who sometimes runs an ensemble called The Groove Commission. He believes that music is a fundamentally human form of communication and also the soundtrack to the tragicomedy that is life. He splits his time between public service, playing tunes, bowling, and chilling on the patio.

Alex Baldoz

Alex Baldoz is an illustrator and fine artist who's work explores different meanings behind the many connections and relations between himself and other people, as well as those between people and the world around them through use of different illustrative tools as well as fabric and materials. Alex represents this through works such as drawing and painting portraits, to smaller installation pieces that create a form of interactivity between multiple viewers.

I desire a connection with another human being. Whether on purpose or by accident, every connection has the power to alter my path of life. While chaos exists in the fabric of time, chance brings together the corners of the cloth we are cut from. How these connections change me can feel apparent, clear as day. They can also be obscure, hidden in darkness.

LIMINAL's graphic design work was done by **Hattie Rensberry**, as part of her internship with Stain'd Arts.

What Do You

"Empathy."

"Unconditional love."

"Everything and Nothing Matters."

"An imperfect God."

"Creativity, magic, love,
vulnerability."

"The guiding spirit of my cunt and
mother nature."

"Possibilities when I can get out of the
way so they can happen."

"Oh my GAWD
the interconnectedness of the
universe
The spaces between."

Believe In?

"Purpose. I believe everyone chooses their own purpose. I
believe in being the example, being the best person I can be for myself and for others. Because there is no higher purpose than service to others."

"I believe that nature is powerful, intelligent and diverse. And rather than try to fix her, we should bow down."

"There is a lot more going on than we humans can perceive. There are so many forces at work. Some are just perceptible enough that we are aware they exists but don't understand."